Jean-Claude Corbeil

Ariane Archambault

# My First
**SPANISH • ENGLISH**
# VISUAL DICTIONARY

FIREFLY BOOKS

# A FIREFLY BOOK

Published by Firefly Books Ltd. 2006

Copyright © 2006 QA International

First printing

**Publisher Cataloging-in-Publication Data (U.S.)**

Corbeil, Jean-Claude.

My first Spanish English visual dictionary/Jean-Claude Corbeil ; Ariane Archambeault.

(80) p. : col. ill. ; cm.

Includes index.

Summary: A general reference visual dictionary for young children featuring terms in English and Spanish.

ISBN-13: 978-1-55407-194-4
ISBN-10: 1-55407-194-1

1. Picture dictionaries, Spanish—Juvenile literature. 2. Picture dictionaries, English—Juvenile literature. 3. Spanish language—Dictionaries—English—Juvenile literature. 4. English language—Dictionaries—Spanish—Juvenile literature. I. Archambeault, Ariane. II. Title.

463.21   dc22   PC4629.C6736   2006

**Library and Archives Canada Cataloguing in Publication**

Corbeil, Jean-Claude, 1932-

My first Spanish/English visual dictionary/Jean-Claude Corbeil, Ariane Archambault.

Includes index.

ISBN-13: 978-1-55407-194-4
ISBN-10: 1-55407-194-1

1. Picture dictionaries, Spanish—Juvenile literature. 2. Picture dictionaries, English—Juvenile literature. 3. Spanish language—Dictionaries, Juvenile—English. 4. English language—Dictionaries, Juvenile—Spanish. I. Archambault, Ariane, 1936- II. Title.

AG250.C66387 2006   j463'.21   C2006-900748-9

Published in the United States by
Firefly Books (U.S.) Inc.
P.O. Box 1338, Ellicott Station
Buffalo, New York  14205

Published in Canada by
Firefly Books Ltd.
66 Leek Crescent
Richmond Hill, Ontario
L4B 1H1

Printed in Singapore

*My First Visual Dictionary was created and produced by :*
**QA International**
329 de la Commune St. West
3rd floor
H2Y 2E1 Canada
T 514.499.3000  F 514.499.3010
www.qa-international.com

**AUTHORS**
Jean-Claude Corbeil
Ariane Archambault

**PUBLISHER**
Caroline Fortin

**EDITORIAL DIRECTORS**
François Fortin
Martine Podesto

**EDITOR-IN-CHIEF**
Anne Rouleau

**TERMINOLOGICAL RESEARCH**
Jean Beaumont
Catherine Briand
Nathalie Guillo

**GRAPHIC DESIGN**
Éric Millette

**COVER AND PAGE SETUP**
Josée Noiseux

**ILLUSTRATION**
**Art Director :** Jocelyn Gardner
Carl Pelletier
Alain Lemire
Jean-Yves Ahern
Pascal Bilodeau
Yan Bohler
Mélanie Boivin
François Escalmel
Rielle Lévesque
Anouk Noël
Michel Rouleau
Claude Thivierge
Mamadou Togola

**DOCUMENTATION**
Stéphanie Lanctôt
Gilles Vézina

**DATA MANAGEMENT**
**Programmer:** Éric Gagnon
Josée Gagnon

**REVISION**
Liliane Michaud

**PRODUCTION**
Nathalie Fréchette

**PREPRESS**
Guylaine Houle
Pascal Goyette
Sophie Pellerin
Kien Tang

**PEDAGOGICAL ADVISER**
Roch Turbide

# Contents

# The body
## El cuerpo

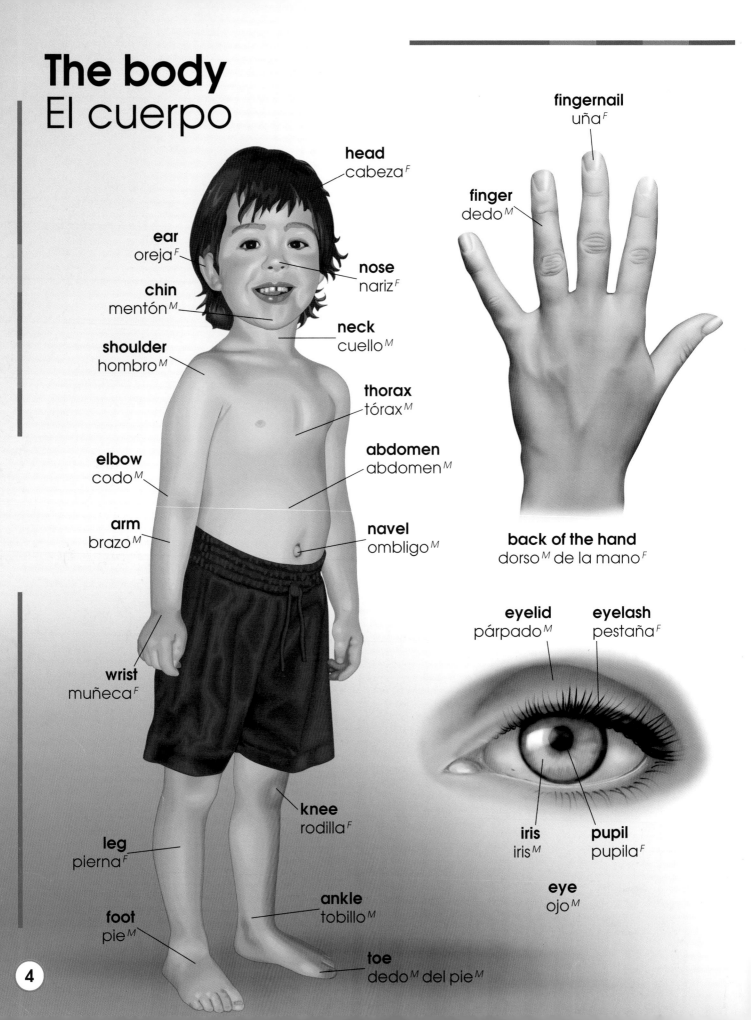

**fingernail**
uña<sup>F</sup>

**head**
cabeza<sup>F</sup>

**finger**
dedo<sup>M</sup>

**ear**
oreja<sup>F</sup>

**nose**
nariz<sup>F</sup>

**chin**
mentón<sup>M</sup>

**neck**
cuello<sup>M</sup>

**shoulder**
hombro<sup>M</sup>

**thorax**
tórax<sup>M</sup>

**abdomen**
abdomen<sup>M</sup>

**elbow**
codo<sup>M</sup>

**back of the hand**
dorso<sup>M</sup> de la mano<sup>F</sup>

**arm**
brazo<sup>M</sup>

**navel**
ombligo<sup>M</sup>

**wrist**
muñeca<sup>F</sup>

**eyelid**
párpado<sup>M</sup>

**eyelash**
pestaña<sup>F</sup>

**knee**
rodilla<sup>F</sup>

**leg**
pierna<sup>F</sup>

**iris**
iris<sup>M</sup>

**pupil**
pupila<sup>F</sup>

**ankle**
tobillo<sup>M</sup>

**eye**
ojo<sup>M</sup>

**foot**
pie<sup>M</sup>

**toe**
dedo<sup>M</sup> del pie<sup>M</sup>

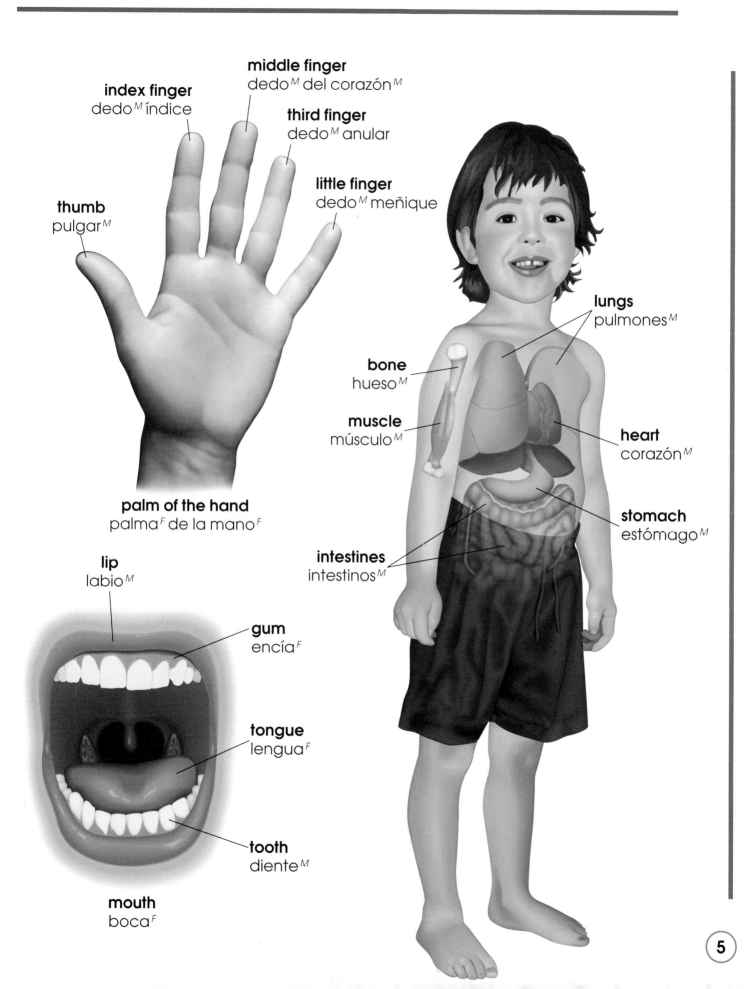

**index finger**
dedo<sup>M</sup> índice

**middle finger**
dedo<sup>M</sup> del corazón<sup>M</sup>

**third finger**
dedo<sup>M</sup> anular

**thumb**
pulgar<sup>M</sup>

**little finger**
dedo<sup>M</sup> meñique

**lungs**
pulmones<sup>M</sup>

**bone**
hueso<sup>M</sup>

**muscle**
músculo<sup>M</sup>

**heart**
corazón<sup>M</sup>

**palm of the hand**
palma<sup>F</sup> de la mano<sup>F</sup>

**stomach**
estómago<sup>M</sup>

**intestines**
intestinos<sup>M</sup>

**lip**
labio<sup>M</sup>

**gum**
encía<sup>F</sup>

**tongue**
lengua<sup>F</sup>

**tooth**
diente<sup>M</sup>

**mouth**
boca<sup>F</sup>

# The body in motion
## El cuerpo en movimiento

**sit**
sentado

**walk**
caminar

**run**
correr

**jump**
saltar

**crawl**
gatear

**sleep**
dormir

**tunnel**
túnel$^M$

**slide**
tobogán$^M$

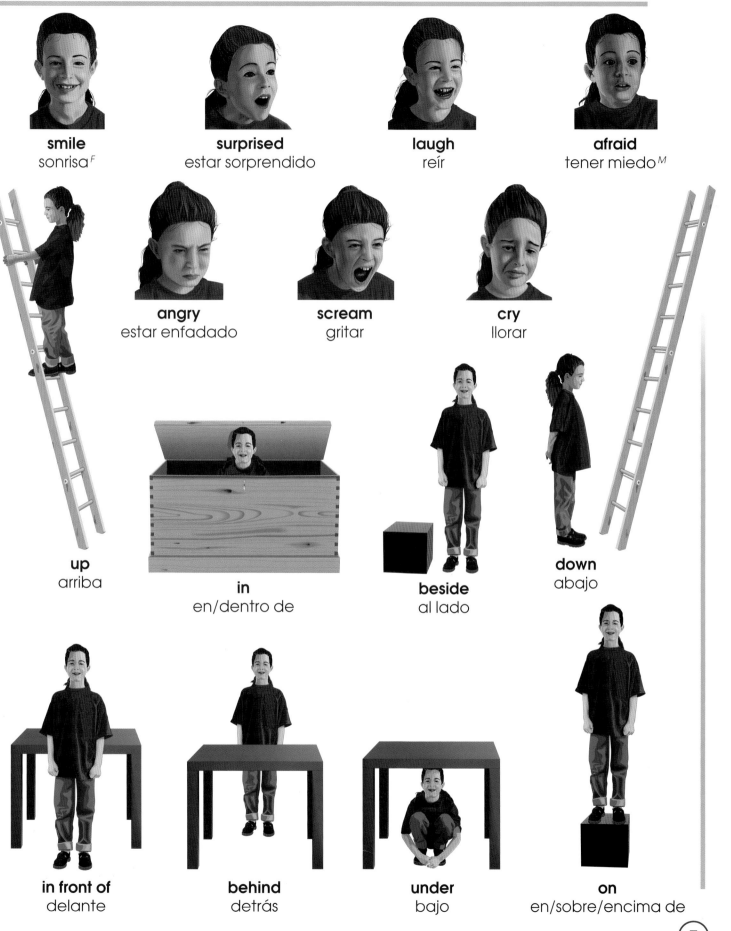

**smile**
sonrisa*F*

**surprised**
estar sorprendido

**laugh**
reír

**afraid**
tener miedo*M*

**angry**
estar enfadado

**scream**
gritar

**cry**
llorar

**up**
arriba

**in**
en/dentro de

**beside**
al lado

**down**
abajo

**in front of**
delante

**behind**
detrás

**under**
bajo

**on**
en/sobre/encima de

# Clothing
## La ropa

**running shoe**
zapatilla<sup>F</sup> deportiva

**tongue**
lengüeta<sup>F</sup>

**shoelace**
cordón<sup>M</sup>

**heel**
talón<sup>M</sup>

**sole**
suela<sup>F</sup>

**strap**
tirante<sup>M</sup>

**anorak**
anorak<sup>M</sup>

**fly**
bragueta<sup>F</sup>

**overalls**
pantalón<sup>M</sup> peto<sup>M</sup>

**sandal**
sandalia<sup>F</sup>

**cardigan**
chaqueta<sup>F</sup> de punto<sup>M</sup>

**turtleneck**
jersey<sup>M</sup> de cuello<sup>M</sup>
de tortuga<sup>F</sup>

**skirt**
falda<sup>F</sup>

**knit shirt**
polo<sup>M</sup>

**T-shirt**
camiseta<sup>F</sup>

**jeans**
vaqueros<sup>M</sup>

**dress**
vestido<sup>M</sup>

**necktie**
corbata<sup>F</sup>

**belt**
cinturón<sup>M</sup>

**briefs**
calzoncillos<sup>M</sup>

**gloves**
guantes<sup>M</sup>

**boxer shorts**
calzoncillos<sup>M</sup>

**shirt**
camisa<sup>F</sup>

**collar**
cuello<sup>M</sup>

**sleeve**
manga<sup>F</sup>

**pocket**
bolsillo<sup>M</sup>

**button**
botón<sup>M</sup>

**swimming trunks**
traje<sup>M</sup> de baño<sup>M</sup>

**swimsuit**
traje<sup>M</sup> de baño<sup>M</sup>

**pajamas**
pijama<sup>M</sup>

**socks**
calcetines<sup>M</sup>

**shorts**
pantalóns<sup>M</sup> cortos

**knitted cap**
gorro<sup>M</sup>

**sweatshirt**
sudadera<sup>F</sup>

**sweatpants**
pantalones<sup>M</sup> de chándal<sup>M</sup>

**snowsuit**
traje<sup>M</sup> de nieve<sup>F</sup>

**scarf**
bufanda<sup>F</sup>

**mitten**
manoplas<sup>M</sup>

**boot**
bota<sup>F</sup>

# At home
## En casa

**edger**
podadora$^F$ de bordes$^M$

**rake**
rastrillo$^M$

**tool box**
caja$^F$ de herramientas$^F$

**hammer**
martillo$^M$

**screwdriver**
destornillador$^M$

**garden hose**
manguera$^F$

**hose trolley**
carretilla$^F$ para manguera$^F$

**wheelbarrow**
carretilla$^F$

**lawn rake**
rastrillo$^M$

**sprinkler**
aspersor$^M$

**garbage can**
cubo$^M$ de basura$^F$

**shed**
cobertizo$^M$

**vegetable garden**
huerto$^M$

**stepladder**
escalera$^F$ de tijera$^F$

**fence**
vallado$^M$

**lawn**
césped$^M$

**mower**
cortacésped$^F$

**playset**
centro<sup>M</sup> de juego<sup>M</sup>

**trapeze**
trapecio<sup>M</sup>

**tricycle**
triciclo<sup>M</sup>

**bucket swing**
barca<sup>F</sup>

**swing**
columpio<sup>M</sup>

**slide**
tobogán<sup>M</sup>

**glider swing**
balancín<sup>M</sup>

**above-ground swimming pool**
piscina<sup>F</sup> elevada

**wagon**
vagón<sup>M</sup>

**ball**
pelota<sup>F</sup>

**in-ground swimming pool**
piscina<sup>F</sup> enterrada

**roof**
tejado<sup>M</sup>

**garage**
garaje<sup>M</sup>

**chimney**
chimenea<sup>F</sup>

**window**
ventana<sup>F</sup>

**sandbox**
arenero<sup>M</sup>

**door**
puerta<sup>F</sup>

**hedge**
seto<sup>M</sup>

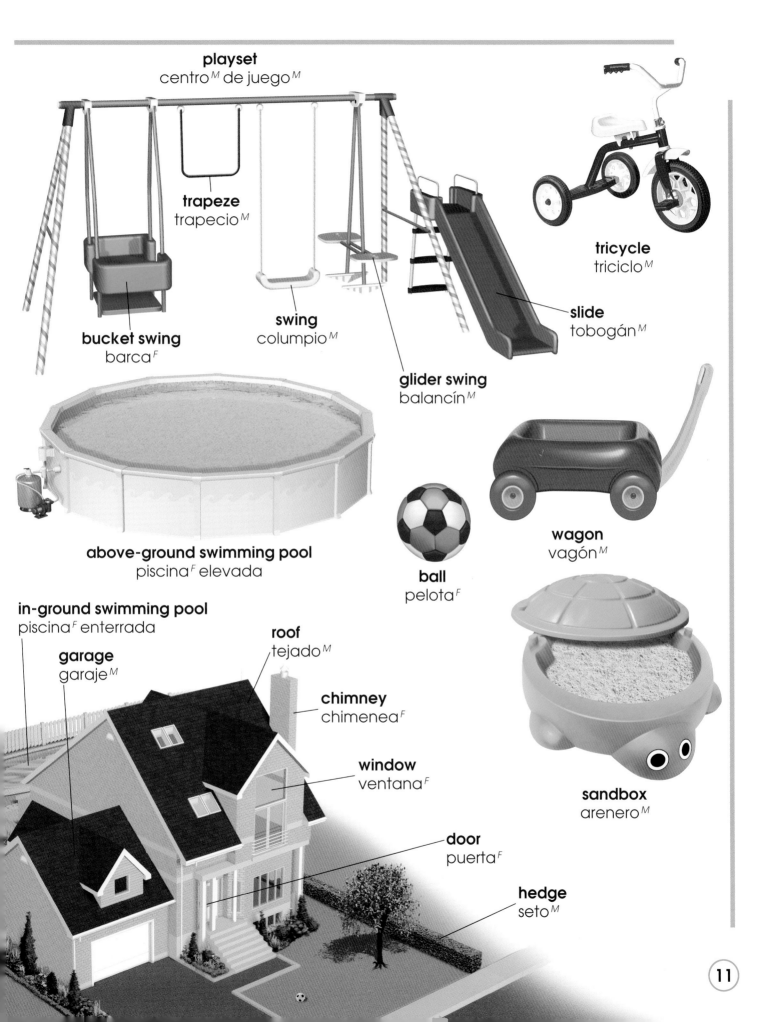

# The bedroom
## La habitación

**jewel box**
joyero$^M$

**music box**
caja$^F$ de música$^F$

**mobile**
carrusel$^M$

**hanger**
percha$^F$

**changing table**
cambiador$^M$

**alarm clock**
despertador$^M$

**mirror**
espejo$^M$

**crib**
cuna$^F$

**playpen**
cuna$^F$ plegable

**headboard**
cabecera$^F$

**curtain**
cortina$^F$

**footboard**
pie$^M$ de la cama$^F$

**table lamp**
lámpara$^F$ de mesa$^F$

CIRCUS

**poster**
cartel$^M$

**pillow**
almohada$^F$

**teddy bear**
osito$^M$ de peluche$^M$

**flat sheet**
sábana$^F$

**dresser**
cómoda$^F$

**comforter**
edredón$^M$

**rug**
alfombra$^F$

**CD-radio-cassette player**
radiocasete<sup>M</sup> con CD<sup>M</sup>

**cassette**
casete<sup>F</sup>

**ceiling fixture**
plafón<sup>M</sup>

**personal stereo**
CD<sup>M</sup> portátil

**compact disc**
disco<sup>M</sup> compacto

**rocking chair**
mecedora<sup>F</sup>

**chiffonier**
chifonier<sup>M</sup>

**bedside table**
mesilla<sup>F</sup> de noche<sup>F</sup>

**linen chest**
baúl<sup>M</sup>

**coat hooks**
perchero<sup>M</sup> de pared<sup>F</sup>

**laundry basket**
cesta<sup>F</sup> de ropa<sup>F</sup>

**wardrobe**
ropero<sup>M</sup>

**slipper**
zapatillas<sup>F</sup>

**door**
puerta<sup>F</sup>

13

# The bathroom
## El cuarto de baño

cotton applicators
aplicadores<sup>M</sup> de algodón<sup>M</sup>

sponge
esponja<sup>F</sup>

dental floss
hilo<sup>M</sup> dental

toothpaste
dentífrico<sup>M</sup>

shampoo
champú<sup>M</sup>

soap
jabón<sup>M</sup>

toothbrush
cepillo<sup>M</sup> de dientes<sup>M</sup>

bubble bath
gel<sup>M</sup> de baño<sup>M</sup>

adhesive bandage
tirita<sup>F</sup>

shower curtain
cortina<sup>F</sup> de ducha<sup>F</sup>

nail clippers
cortaúñas<sup>M</sup>

mouthwash
enjuague<sup>M</sup>
bucal

bathtub
bañera<sup>F</sup>

tissues
pañuelos<sup>M</sup>

medicine cabinet
armario<sup>M</sup> botiquín<sup>M</sup>

toilet paper
papel<sup>M</sup> higiénico

faucet
grifo<sup>M</sup>

sink
lavabo<sup>M</sup>

toilet
inodoro<sup>M</sup>

bathroom scale
báscula<sup>F</sup> de baño<sup>M</sup>

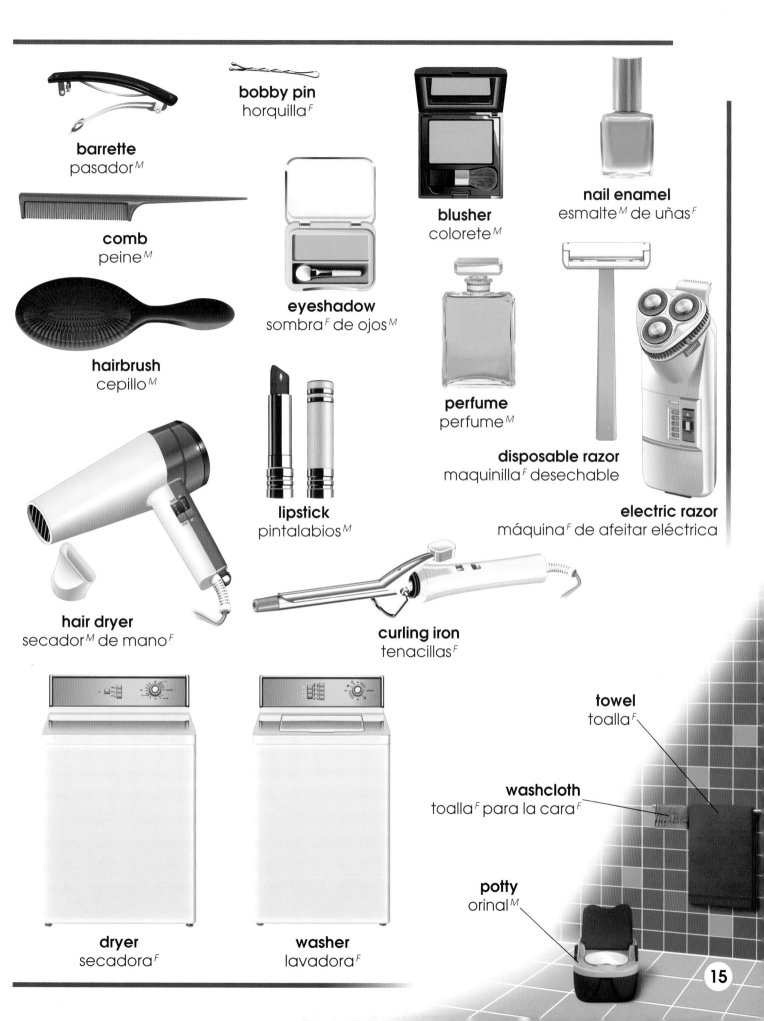

**barrette**
pasador<sup>M</sup>

**bobby pin**
horquilla<sup>F</sup>

**blusher**
colorete<sup>M</sup>

**nail enamel**
esmalte<sup>M</sup> de uñas<sup>F</sup>

**comb**
peine<sup>M</sup>

**eyeshadow**
sombra<sup>F</sup> de ojos<sup>M</sup>

**hairbrush**
cepillo<sup>M</sup>

**perfume**
perfume<sup>M</sup>

**disposable razor**
maquinilla<sup>F</sup> desechable

**electric razor**
máquina<sup>F</sup> de afeitar eléctrica

**lipstick**
pintalabios<sup>M</sup>

**hair dryer**
secador<sup>M</sup> de mano<sup>F</sup>

**curling iron**
tenacillas<sup>F</sup>

**towel**
toalla<sup>F</sup>

**washcloth**
toalla<sup>F</sup> para la cara<sup>F</sup>

**potty**
orinal<sup>M</sup>

**dryer**
secadora<sup>F</sup>

**washer**
lavadora<sup>F</sup>

# The living room
## El salón

**fan**
ventilador<sup>M</sup>

**shade**
pantalla<sup>F</sup>

**ottoman**
puf<sup>M</sup>

**armchair**
silla<sup>F</sup> de brazos<sup>M</sup>

**futon**
futón<sup>M</sup>

**grandfather clock**
reloj<sup>M</sup> de péndulo<sup>M</sup>

**sofa bed**
sofá cama<sup>M</sup>

**folding chairs**
sillas<sup>F</sup> plegables

**base**
base<sup>F</sup>

**floor lamp**
lámpara<sup>F</sup> de pie<sup>M</sup>

**sofa**
sofá<sup>M</sup>

**fireplace**
chimenea<sup>F</sup>

**love seat**
sofá<sup>M</sup> de dos plazas<sup>F</sup>

**cushion**
cojín<sup>M</sup>

**table**
mesa<sup>F</sup>

**television set**
televisor<sup>M</sup>

**DVD player**
lector<sup>M</sup> de DVD<sup>M</sup>

**DVD**
DVD<sup>M</sup>

**remote control**
mando<sup>M</sup> a distancia<sup>F</sup>

**videocassette**
cinta<sup>F</sup> de vídeo<sup>M</sup>

**videocassette recorder (VCR)**
reproductor/grabador de video<sup>M</sup> VCR

**mini stereo sound system**
mini-cadena<sup>F</sup> estéreo

**compact disc player**
lector de disco<sup>M</sup> compacto

**telephone**
teléfono<sup>M</sup>

**headphones**
auriculares<sup>M</sup>

**book**
libro<sup>M</sup>

**bookcase**
librería<sup>F</sup>

**cassette player**
lector<sup>M</sup> de casetes<sup>F</sup>

**speaker**
altavoz<sup>M</sup>

**fire irons**
utensilios<sup>M</sup> para la chimenea<sup>F</sup>

**log carrier**
portaleños<sup>M</sup>

# The playroom
## La sala de juegos

**drawing board**
pizarra<sup>F</sup>

**rattle**
sonajero<sup>M</sup>

**toy cars**
cochecitos<sup>M</sup>

**modeling clay**
plastilina<sup>F</sup>

**toy garage**
garaje<sup>M</sup>

**assembly toy**
muñeco<sup>M</sup> rompecabezas<sup>M</sup>

**toy train**
tren<sup>M</sup> en miniatura<sup>F</sup>

**interlocking blocks**
ladrillos<sup>M</sup>

**doll**
muñeca<sup>F</sup>

**rocking horse**
caballo<sup>M</sup> balancín<sup>M</sup>

**walker**
andador<sup>M</sup>

**stroller**
sillita<sup>F</sup>

**workbench**
banco<sup>M</sup> de trabajo<sup>M</sup>

**blocks**
cubos<sup>M</sup>

**spinning top**
peonza<sup>F</sup>

**peg puzzle**
rompecabezas<sup>M</sup>

**stackable rings**
aros<sup>M</sup> apilables

**felt tip pen**
rotulador$^M$

**brush**
pincel$^M$

**adhesive tape**
cinta$^F$ adhesiva

**watercolor paints**
pastillas$^F$ de acuarela$^F$

**scissors**
tijeras$^F$ de modista$^F$

**glue stick**
lápiz$^M$ adhesivo

**crayons**
ceras$^F$

**easel**
caballete$^M$

**colored pencils**
lápices$^M$ de colores$^M$

**memo pad**
libreta$^F$

**cards**
baraja$^F$

**die**
dado$^M$

**dominoes**
dominó$^M$

**monitor**
pantalla$^F$

**darts**
juego$^M$ de dardos$^M$

**game console**
consola$^F$ de juego$^M$

**controller**
mando$^M$

**soccer table**
futbolín$^M$

**video entertainment system**
videojuego$^M$

# The kitchen
## La cocina

**toaster**
tostador$^M$

**kettle**
hervidor$^M$

**coffeemaker**
cafetera$^F$

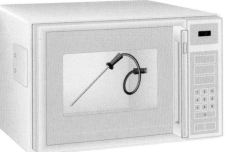

**microwave oven**
horno$^M$ microondas

**colander**
escurridor$^M$

**blender**
licuadora$^F$

**hand mixer**
batidora$^F$ de mano$^F$

**salad spinner**
secadora$^F$ de ensalada$^F$

**mixing bowls**
boles$^M$ para batir

**oven mitt**
manopla$^F$ de cocina$^F$

**apron**
delantal$^M$

**freezer**
congelador$^M$

**cabinet**
armario$^M$

**sink**
fregadero$^M$

**refrigerator**
frigorífico$^M$

**dishwasher**
lavavajillas$^F$

**drawer**
cajón$^M$

**funnel**
embudo<sup>M</sup>

**kitchen timer**
minutero<sup>M</sup>

**scouring pad**
estropajo<sup>M</sup> con esponja<sup>F</sup>

**tea towel**
bayeta<sup>F</sup> de cocina<sup>F</sup>

**measuring spoons**
cucharas<sup>F</sup> dosificadoras

**measuring cup**
jarra<sup>F</sup> medidora

**corkscrew**
sacacorchos<sup>M</sup>

**ice-cream scoop**
cuchara<sup>F</sup> para helado<sup>M</sup>

**cookie cutters**
moldes<sup>M</sup> de pastas<sup>F</sup>

**peeler**
pelapatatas<sup>M</sup>

**grater**
rallador<sup>M</sup>

**can opener**
abrelatas<sup>M</sup>

**kitchen knife**
cuchillo<sup>M</sup> de cocina<sup>F</sup>

**citrus juicer**
exprimidor<sup>M</sup>

**cutting board**
tabla<sup>F</sup> de cortar

**pie pan**
molde<sup>M</sup> para tartas<sup>F</sup>

**rolling pin**
rodillo<sup>M</sup>

**electric range**
cocina<sup>F</sup> eléctrica

**frying pan**
sartén<sup>F</sup>

**surface element**
hornillo<sup>M</sup>

**saucepan**
cacerola<sup>F</sup>

**oven**
horno<sup>M</sup>

**stock pot**
olla<sup>F</sup>

**baking sheet**
bandeja<sup>F</sup> de pastelería<sup>F</sup>

**muffin pan**
molde<sup>M</sup> para magdalenas<sup>F</sup>

# The meal
## La comida

**spouted cup**
taza<sup>F</sup> de boquilla<sup>F</sup>

**cup**
taza<sup>F</sup>

**wineglass**
copa<sup>F</sup> de vino<sup>M</sup>

**small decanter**
decantador<sup>M</sup>

**butter dish**
mantequera<sup>F</sup>

**teapot**
tetera<sup>F</sup>

**sugar bowl**
azucarero<sup>M</sup>

**creamer**
jarrita<sup>F</sup> de leche<sup>F</sup>

**ramekin**
cuenco<sup>M</sup> de queso<sup>M</sup>
blando

**water pitcher**
jarra<sup>F</sup> de agua<sup>F</sup>

**salad bowl**
ensaladera<sup>F</sup>

**soup bowl**
escudilla<sup>F</sup>

**glass**
vaso<sup>M</sup>

**knife**
cuchillo<sup>M</sup>

**gravy boat**
salsera<sup>F</sup>

**spoon**
cuchara<sup>F</sup>

**napkin**
servilleta<sup>F</sup>

**tablecloth**
mantel<sup>M</sup>

**soup tureen**
sopera<sup>F</sup>

**flour**
harina<sup>F</sup>

**sandwich**
sándwich<sup>M</sup>

**salad**
ensalada<sup>F</sup>

**steak**
bistec<sup>F</sup> / filete<sup>M</sup>

**sugar**
azúcar<sup>M/F</sup>

**pizza**
pizza<sup>M</sup>

**turkey**
pavo<sup>M</sup>

**fish**
pescado<sup>M</sup>

**brown sugar**
azúcar<sup>M</sup> moreno

**stew**
guiso<sup>M</sup>

**cereal**
cereales<sup>M</sup>

**spaghetti**
espagueti<sup>M</sup>

**maple syrup**
jarabe<sup>M</sup> de arce<sup>M</sup>

**honey**
miel<sup>M</sup>

**cookies**
galletas<sup>F</sup>

**ice cream**
helado<sup>M</sup>

**pie**
tarta<sup>F</sup>

**plate**
plato<sup>M</sup>

**salt shaker**
salero<sup>M</sup>

**fork**
tenedor<sup>M</sup>

**bun**
bollo<sup>M</sup>

**pepper mill**
molinillo<sup>M</sup> de
pimienta<sup>F</sup>

**cake**
pastel<sup>M</sup>

# Vegetables
## El huerto y las hortalizas

**artichoke**
alcachofa*F*

**lettuce**
lechuga*F*

**cauliflower**
coliflor*F*

**spinach**
espinaca*F*

**asparagus**
espárrago*M*

**rhubarb**
ruibarbo*M*

**cabbage**
col*F*

**fennel**
hinojo*M*

**broccoli**
brécol*M*

**celery**
apio*M*

**brussels sprouts**
coles*F* de Bruselas

**carrot**
zanahoria*F*

**turnip**
nabo*M*

**potatoes**
patatas*F*

**parsnip**
chirivía*F*

**beet**
remolacha*F*

**radish**
rábano*M*

**rutabaga**
nabo*M* sueco

**sweet potato**
batata*F*

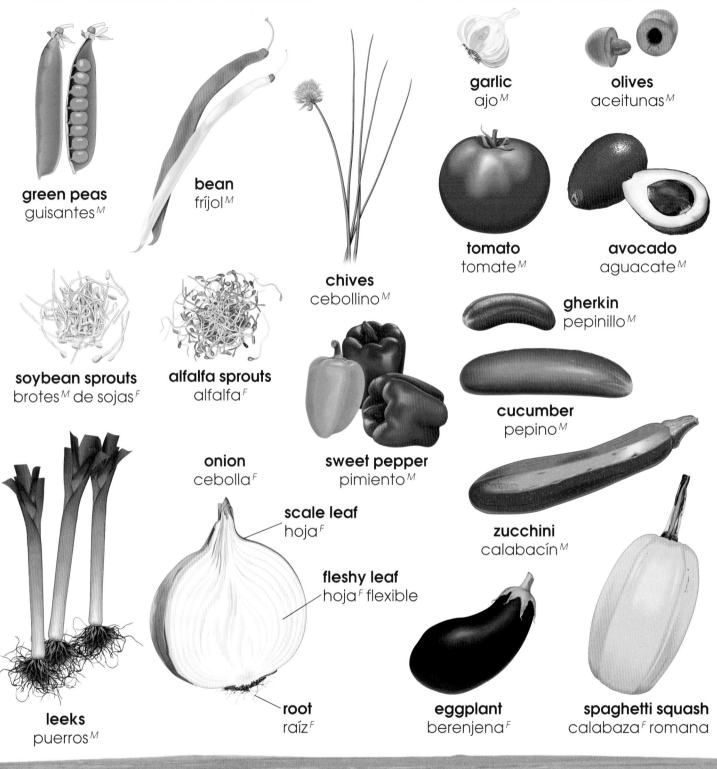

**green peas**
guisantes $^M$

**bean**
fríjol $^M$

**chives**
cebollino $^M$

**garlic**
ajo $^M$

**olives**
aceitunas $^M$

**tomato**
tomate $^M$

**avocado**
aguacate $^M$

**soybean sprouts**
brotes $^M$ de sojas $^F$

**alfalfa sprouts**
alfalfa $^F$

**gherkin**
pepinillo $^M$

**cucumber**
pepino $^M$

**sweet pepper**
pimiento $^M$

**onion**
cebolla $^F$

**zucchini**
calabacín $^M$

**scale leaf**
hoja $^F$

**fleshy leaf**
hoja $^F$ flexible

**root**
raíz $^F$

**leeks**
puerros $^M$

**eggplant**
berenjena $^F$

**spaghetti squash**
calabaza $^F$ romana

# Fruits
## Las frutas

**pear**
pera$^F$

**banana**
banana$^F$

**lime**
lima$^M$

**lemon**
limón$^M$

### section of an apple
corte$^M$ de una manzana$^F$

**stem**
rabillo$^M$

**skin**
piel$^F$

**seed**
pepita$^F$

**peach**
melocotón$^M$

**nectarine**
nectarina$^F$

**muskmelon**
melón$^M$ escrito

**grapefruit**
pomelo$^M$

**honeydew melon**
melón$^M$ de miel

**apricot**
albaricoque$^M$

**plums**
ciruelas$^F$

**orange**
naranja$^F$

**apple**
manzana$^F$

**strawberries**
fresas$^F$

**blueberries**
arándanos$^M$

26

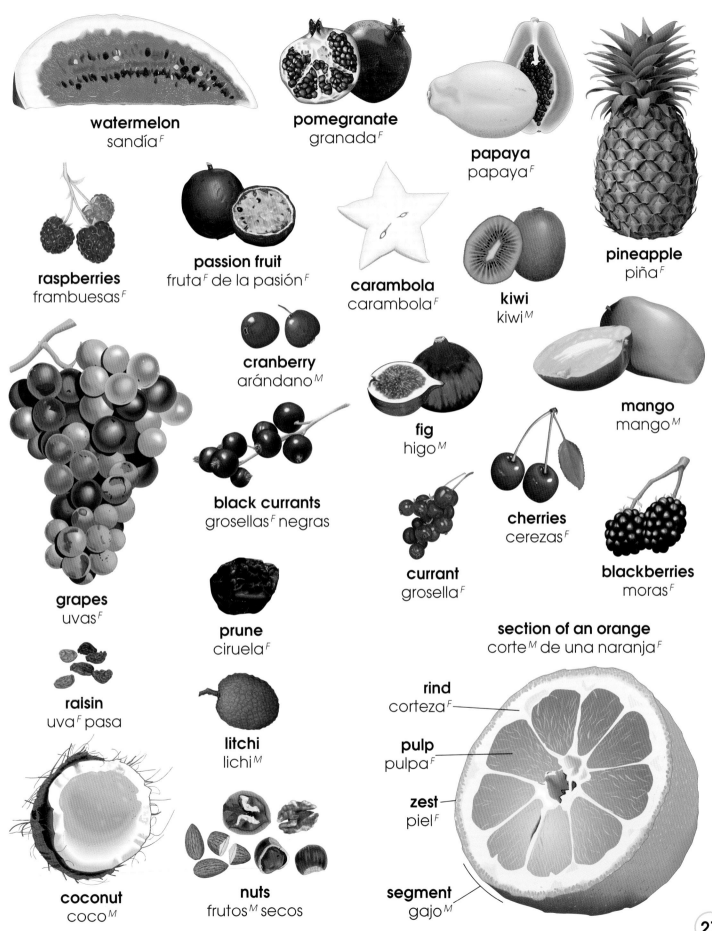

**watermelon**
sandía<sup>F</sup>

**pomegranate**
granada<sup>F</sup>

**papaya**
papaya<sup>F</sup>

**pineapple**
piña<sup>F</sup>

**raspberries**
frambuesas<sup>F</sup>

**passion fruit**
fruta<sup>F</sup> de la pasión<sup>F</sup>

**carambola**
carambola<sup>F</sup>

**kiwi**
kiwi<sup>M</sup>

**cranberry**
arándano<sup>M</sup>

**fig**
higo<sup>M</sup>

**mango**
mango<sup>M</sup>

**grapes**
uvas<sup>F</sup>

**black currants**
grosellas<sup>F</sup> negras

**currant**
grosella<sup>F</sup>

**cherries**
cerezas<sup>F</sup>

**blackberries**
moras<sup>F</sup>

**raisin**
uva<sup>F</sup> pasa

**prune**
ciruela<sup>F</sup>

**litchi**
lichi<sup>M</sup>

**section of an orange**
corte<sup>M</sup> de una naranja<sup>F</sup>

rind
corteza<sup>F</sup>

pulp
pulpa<sup>F</sup>

zest
piel<sup>F</sup>

**coconut**
coco<sup>M</sup>

**nuts**
frutos<sup>M</sup> secos

segment
gajo<sup>M</sup>

# The supermarket
# El supermercado

**pasta**
pasta<sup>F</sup>

**tortillas**
tortillas<sup>F</sup>

**pita bread**
pan<sup>M</sup> de pita<sup>F</sup>

**white bread**
pan<sup>M</sup> blanco

**baguette**
baguette<sup>F</sup>

**bagel**
rosquilla<sup>F</sup>

**croissant**
cruasán<sup>M</sup>

**rice**
arroz<sup>M</sup>

**egg carton**
cajas<sup>F</sup> de cartón<sup>M</sup> para huevos<sup>M</sup>

**egg**
huevo<sup>M</sup>

**milk carton**
cartón<sup>M</sup> de leche<sup>F</sup>

**ice cream cup**
tarrina<sup>F</sup> de helado<sup>M</sup>

**yogurt**
vaso<sup>M</sup> de yogur<sup>M</sup>

**cheese**
queso<sup>M</sup>

**baby food**
tarros<sup>M</sup>
pequeños

**butter**
mantequilla<sup>M</sup>

**freezer bag**
bolsa<sup>F</sup> para congelados<sup>M</sup>

**spices**
especias<sup>F</sup>

**bag of cookies**
bolsa<sup>F</sup> de galletas<sup>F</sup>

**fruit juice**
zumo<sup>M</sup> de fruta<sup>F</sup>

**food can**
lata<sup>F</sup> de conserva<sup>F</sup>

**aluminum foil**
papel<sup>M</sup> de aluminio<sup>M</sup>

**plastic film (cellophane)**
papel<sup>M</sup> de celofán

**cash register**
caja<sup>F</sup> registradora

**steak**
bistec$^M$

**sausage**
salchicha$^F$

**lobster**
bogavante$^M$

**chicken**
pollo$^M$

**bacon**
beicon$^M$

**salami**
salami$^M$

**cooked ham**
jamón$^M$ de York

**salmon**
salmón$^M$

**chocolate bar**
tableta$^F$ de chocolate$^M$

**candies**
caramelos$^M$

**mussel**
mejillón$^M$

**counter**
mostrador$^M$ acristalado

**oyster**
ostra$^F$

**ketchup**
ketchup$^M$

**wine vinegar**
vinagre$^M$ de vino$^M$

**olive oil**
aceite$^M$ de oliva$^F$

**shopping cart**
carrito$^M$

**shopping basket**
cesta$^F$ de la compra$^F$

# Familiar animals
## Los animales domésticos

**turtle**
tortuga$^F$

**jar**
pecera$^F$

**budgie**
periquito$^M$

**cage**
jaula$^F$

**goldfish**
pez$^M$ rojo

**hamster**
hámster$^M$

**canary**
canario$^M$

**parrot**
loro$^M$

**guinea pig**
cobaya$^F$

**rat**
rata$^F$

**rabbit**
conejo$^M$

**vivarium**

**chameleon**
camaleón$^M$

**cat**
gato$^M$ doméstico

**branch**
rama$^F$

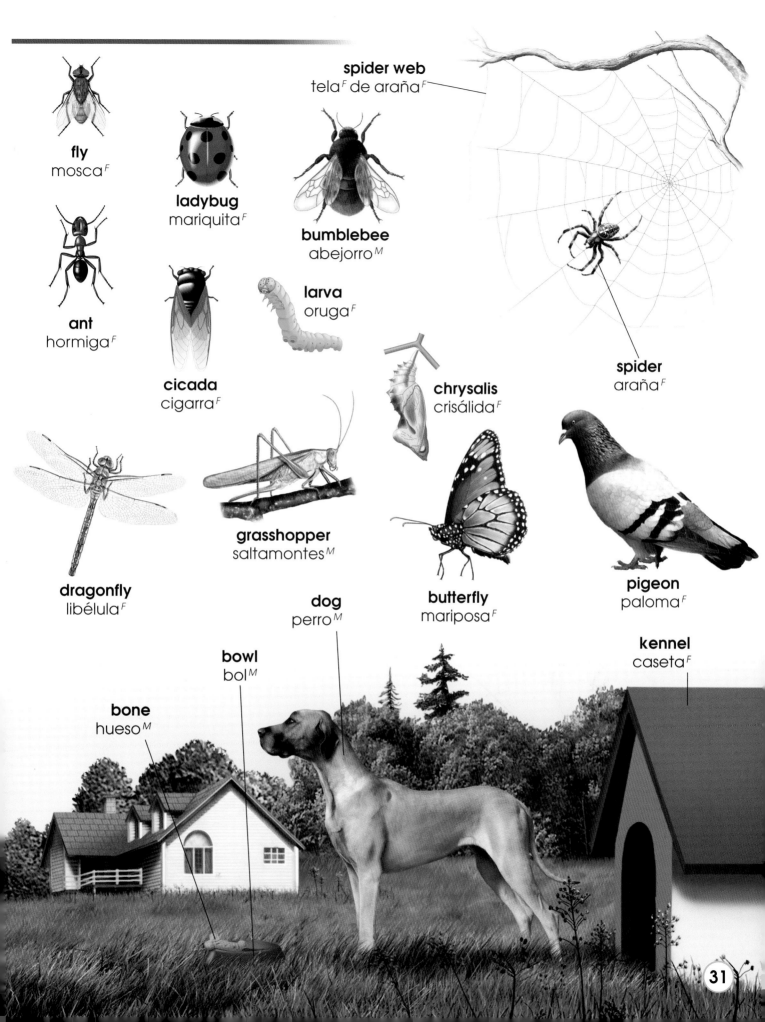

**fly**
mosca^F

**ladybug**
mariquita^F

**spider web**
tela^F de araña^F

**bumblebee**
abejorro^M

**ant**
hormiga^F

**cicada**
cigarra^F

**larva**
oruga^F

**chrysalis**
crisálida^F

**spider**
araña^F

**dragonfly**
libélula^F

**grasshopper**
saltamontes^M

**butterfly**
mariposa^F

**pigeon**
paloma^F

**dog**
perro^M

**bone**
hueso^M

**bowl**
bol^M

**kennel**
caseta^F

31

# The farm
# La granja

**quail**
codorniz*F*

**ostrich**
avestruz*F*

**chick**
polluelo*M*

**hen**
gallina*F*

**turkey**
pavo*M*

**duck**
pato*M*

**goose**
oca*F*

**horse**
caballo*M*

**mane**
crin*F*

**goat**
cabra*F*

**sheep**
oveja*F*

**tail**
cola*F*

**hoof**
casco*M*

**horseshoe**
herradura*F*

**donkey**
asno*M*

**pig**
cerdo*M*

**hen house**
gallinero*M*

**rooster**
gallo*M*

**tractor**
tractor*M*

**cow**
vaca*F*

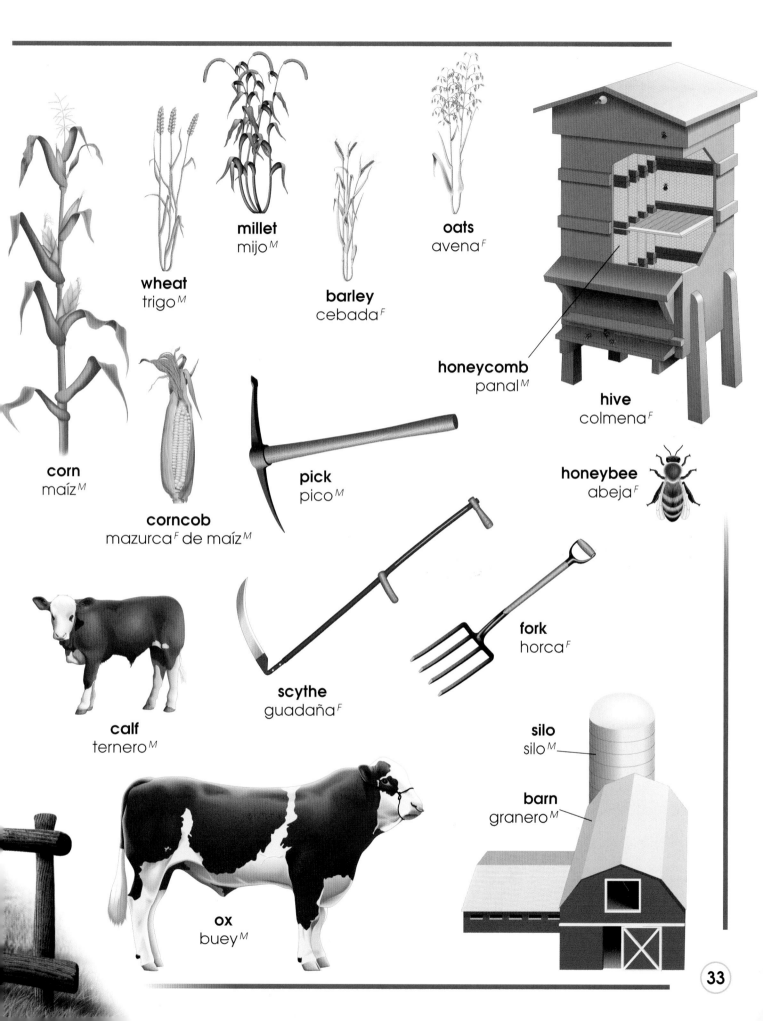

**millet**
mijo<sup>M</sup>

**oats**
avena<sup>F</sup>

**wheat**
trigo<sup>M</sup>

**barley**
cebada<sup>F</sup>

**honeycomb**
panal<sup>M</sup>

**corn**
maíz<sup>M</sup>

**pick**
pico<sup>M</sup>

**hive**
colmena<sup>F</sup>

**honeybee**
abeja<sup>F</sup>

**corncob**
mazurca<sup>F</sup> de maíz<sup>M</sup>

**fork**
horca<sup>F</sup>

**calf**
ternero<sup>M</sup>

**scythe**
guadaña<sup>F</sup>

**silo**
silo<sup>M</sup>

**barn**
granero<sup>M</sup>

**ox**
buey<sup>M</sup>

# The forest
## El bosque

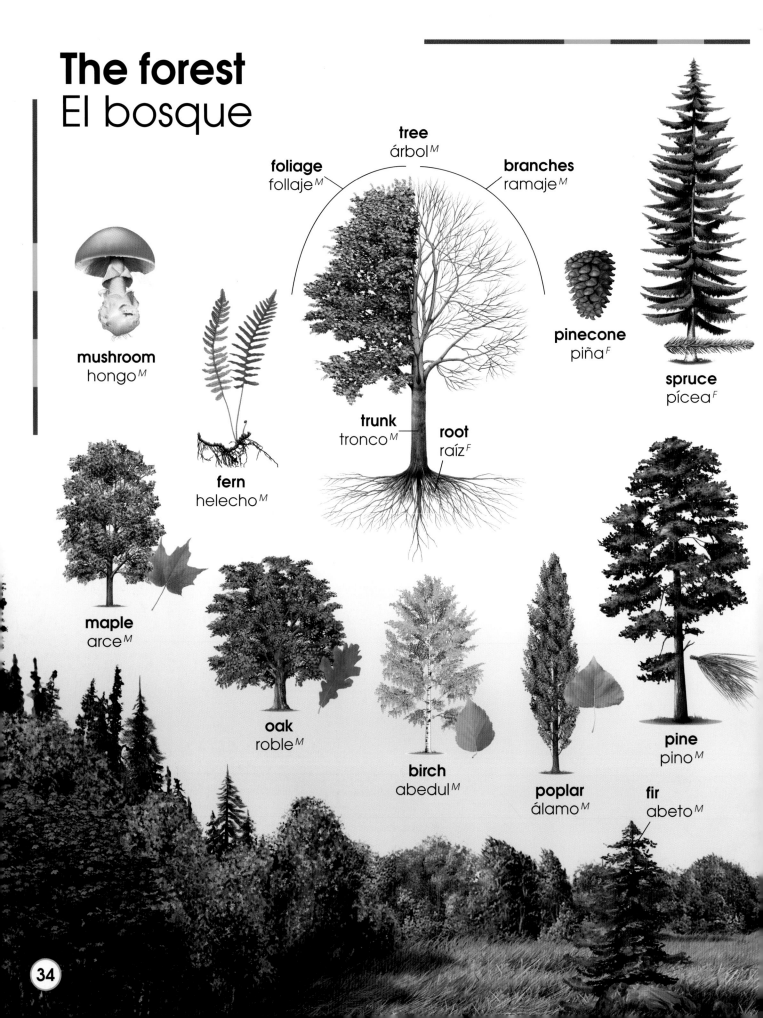

tree
árbol<sup>M</sup>

foliage
follaje<sup>M</sup>

branches
ramaje<sup>M</sup>

pinecone
piña<sup>F</sup>

spruce
pícea<sup>F</sup>

mushroom
hongo<sup>M</sup>

fern
helecho<sup>M</sup>

trunk
tronco<sup>M</sup>

root
raíz<sup>F</sup>

maple
arce<sup>M</sup>

oak
roble<sup>M</sup>

birch
abedul<sup>M</sup>

poplar
álamo<sup>M</sup>

pine
pino<sup>M</sup>

fir
abeto<sup>M</sup>

**sparrow**
gorrión<sup>M</sup>

**jay**
arrendajo<sup>M</sup>

**goldfinch**
jilguero<sup>M</sup>

**owl**
búho<sup>M</sup>

**falcon**
halcón<sup>M</sup>

**woodpecker**
pájaro<sup>M</sup> carpintero

**robin**
petirrojo<sup>M</sup>

**field mouse**
ratón<sup>M</sup> de campo<sup>M</sup>

**frog**
rana<sup>F</sup>

**chipmunk**
ardilla<sup>M</sup> listada

**skunk**
mofeta<sup>M</sup>

**porcupine**
puerco<sup>M</sup> espín

**squirrel**
ardilla<sup>F</sup>

**snake**
culebra<sup>F</sup>

**hare**
liebre<sup>F</sup>

**wolf**
lobo<sup>M</sup>

**beaver**
castor<sup>M</sup>

**moose**
alce<sup>M</sup> americano

**bear**
oso<sup>M</sup>

**deer**
corzo<sup>M</sup>

# The desert and the savanna
## El desierto y la sabana

**tick**
garrapata$^F$

**tarantula**
tarántula$^F$

**jerboa**
jerbo$^M$

**lizard**
lagarto$^M$

**scorpion**
escorpión$^M$

**claw**
pinza$^F$

**vulture**
buitre$^M$

**pouch**
bolsa$^F$

**kangaroo**
canguro$^M$

**rattlesnake**
serpiente$^F$ de cascabel$^M$

**fennec**
fenec$^M$

**dromedary camel**
dromedario$^M$

**bactrian camel**
camello$^M$

**hyena**
hiena[F]

**crocodile**
cocodrilo[M]

**leopard**
leopardo[M]

**giraffe**
jirafa[F]

**tiger**
tigre[M]

**lion**
león[M]

**gorilla**
gorila[M]

**tusk**
colmillo[M]

**hippopotamus**
hipopótamo[M]

**elephant**
elefante[M]

**trunk**
trompa[F]

**antelope**
antílope[M]

**zebra**
cebra[F]

**mongoose**
mangosta[F]

**rhinoceros**
rinoceronte[M]

# The sea
## El mar

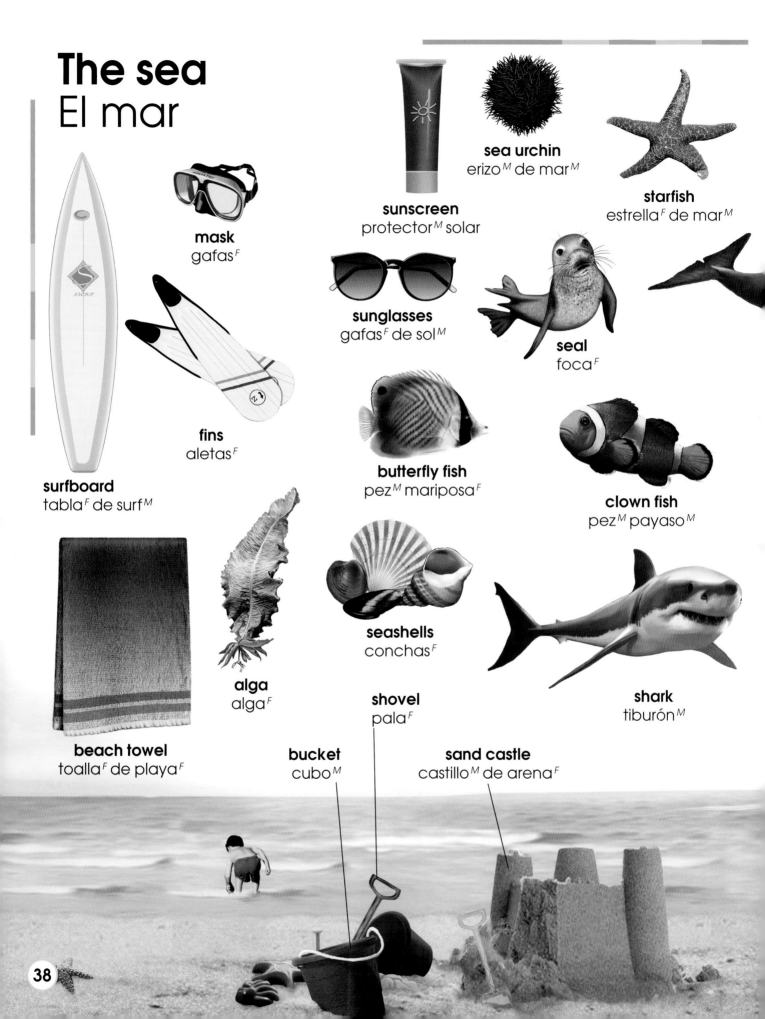

**mask**
gafas<sup>F</sup>

**fins**
aletas<sup>F</sup>

**surfboard**
tabla<sup>F</sup> de surf<sup>M</sup>

**beach towel**
toalla<sup>F</sup> de playa<sup>F</sup>

**alga**
alga<sup>F</sup>

**sunscreen**
protector<sup>M</sup> solar

**sea urchin**
erizo<sup>M</sup> de mar<sup>M</sup>

**starfish**
estrella<sup>F</sup> de mar<sup>M</sup>

**sunglasses**
gafas<sup>F</sup> de sol<sup>M</sup>

**seal**
foca<sup>F</sup>

**butterfly fish**
pez<sup>M</sup> mariposa<sup>F</sup>

**clown fish**
pez<sup>M</sup> payaso<sup>M</sup>

**seashells**
conchas<sup>F</sup>

**shovel**
pala<sup>F</sup>

**shark**
tiburón<sup>M</sup>

**bucket**
cubo<sup>M</sup>

**sand castle**
castillo<sup>M</sup> de arena<sup>F</sup>

**skate**
raya<sup>F</sup>

**sea horse**
caballito<sup>M</sup> de mar<sup>M</sup>

**dolphin**
delfín<sup>F</sup>

**palm tree**
palmera<sup>F</sup>

**crab**
cangrejo<sup>M</sup> de mar<sup>M</sup>

**pelican**
pelícano<sup>M</sup>

**whale**
ballena<sup>F</sup>

**tentacle**
tentáculo<sup>M</sup>

**sucker**
ventosa<sup>F</sup>

**octopus**
pulpo<sup>M</sup>

**beach umbrella**
sombrilla<sup>F</sup>

**gull**
gaviota<sup>F</sup>

39

# Dinosaurs
## Los dinosaurios

**stegosaurus**
stegosaurus[M]

**allosaurus**
allosaurus[M]

**pachycephalosaurus**
pachycephalosaurus

**hadrosaurus**
hadrosaurus[M]

**deinonychus**
deinonychus[M]

**brachiosaurus**
brachiosaurus[M]

**ankylosaurus**
ankylosaurus[M]

**spinosaurus**
spinosaurus*M*

**rhamphorynchus**
rhamphorynchus*M*

**diplodocus**
diplodocus*M*

**parasauroloph**
parasaurolophus*M*

**tyrannosaurus**
tyrannosaurus*M*

**triceratops**
triceratops*M*

# Plants
## Las plantas

**dandelion**
diente<sup>M</sup> de león<sup>M</sup>

**thistle**
cardo<sup>M</sup>

**orchid**
orquídea<sup>F</sup>

**lily of the valley**
muguete<sup>M</sup>

**petal**
pétalo<sup>M</sup>

**carnation**
clavel<sup>M</sup>

**daisy**
margarita<sup>F</sup>

**crocus**
croco<sup>M</sup>

**daffodil**
narciso<sup>M</sup>

**rose**
rosa<sup>F</sup>

**poppy**
amapola<sup>F</sup>

**lily**
azucena<sup>F</sup>

**tulip**
tulipán<sup>M</sup>

**pond**
estanque<sup>M</sup>

**bush**
arbusto<sup>M</sup>

**path**
paseo<sup>M</sup>

**sunflower**
girasol<sup>M</sup>

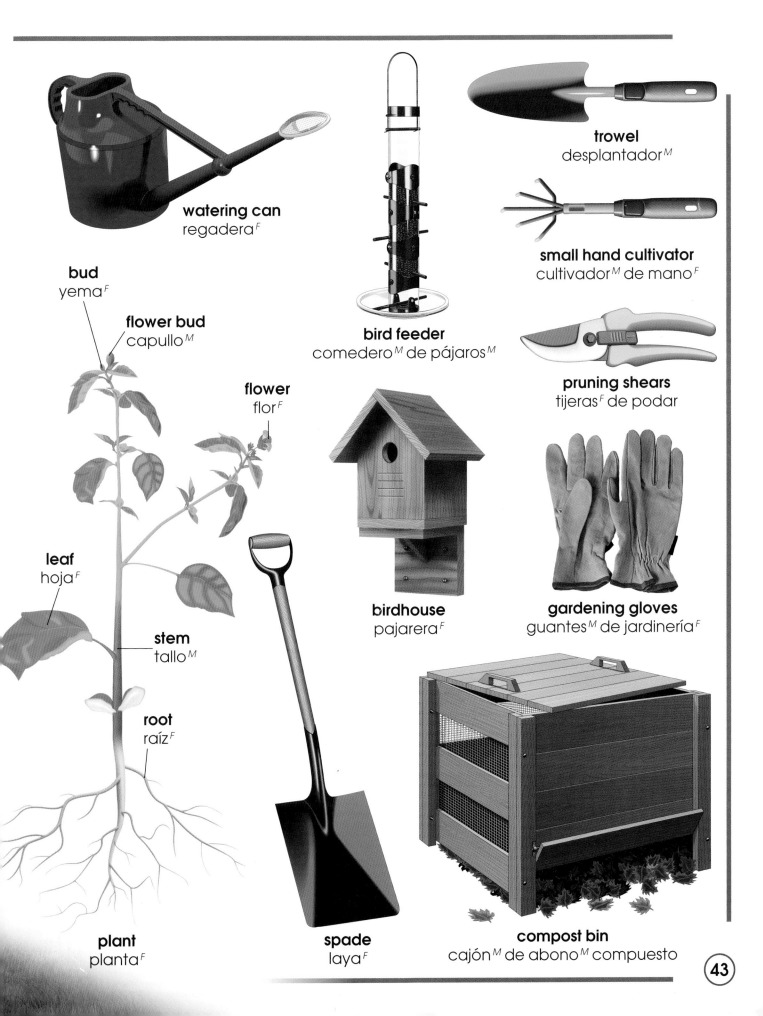

**watering can**
regadera<sup>F</sup>

**bud**
yema<sup>F</sup>

**flower bud**
capullo<sup>M</sup>

**flower**
flor<sup>F</sup>

**bird feeder**
comedero<sup>M</sup> de pájaros<sup>M</sup>

**trowel**
desplantador<sup>M</sup>

**small hand cultivator**
cultivador<sup>M</sup> de mano<sup>F</sup>

**pruning shears**
tijeras<sup>F</sup> de podar

**birdhouse**
pajarera<sup>F</sup>

**gardening gloves**
guantes<sup>M</sup> de jardinería<sup>F</sup>

**leaf**
hoja<sup>F</sup>

**stem**
tallo<sup>M</sup>

**root**
raíz<sup>F</sup>

**plant**
planta<sup>F</sup>

**spade**
laya<sup>F</sup>

**compost bin**
cajón<sup>M</sup> de abono<sup>M</sup> compuesto

# Space
## El espacio

**planetarium**
planetario<sup>M</sup>

**Moon**
Luna<sup>F</sup>

**Hubble space telescope**
telescopio<sup>M</sup> espacial Hubble

**telescope**
telescopio<sup>M</sup>

**new moon**
luna<sup>F</sup> neuva

**crescent moon**
luna<sup>F</sup> creciente

**quarter moon**
cuarto<sup>M</sup> de luna

**full moon**
luna<sup>F</sup> llena

**rocket**
cohete<sup>M</sup>

**Sun**
Sol<sup>M</sup>

**Earth**
Tierra<sup>F</sup>

**asteroid belt**
cinturón<sup>M</sup> de asteroides<sup>M</sup>

**Mercury**
Mercurio

**Venus**
Venus

**Mars**
Marte

**Jupiter**
Júpiter

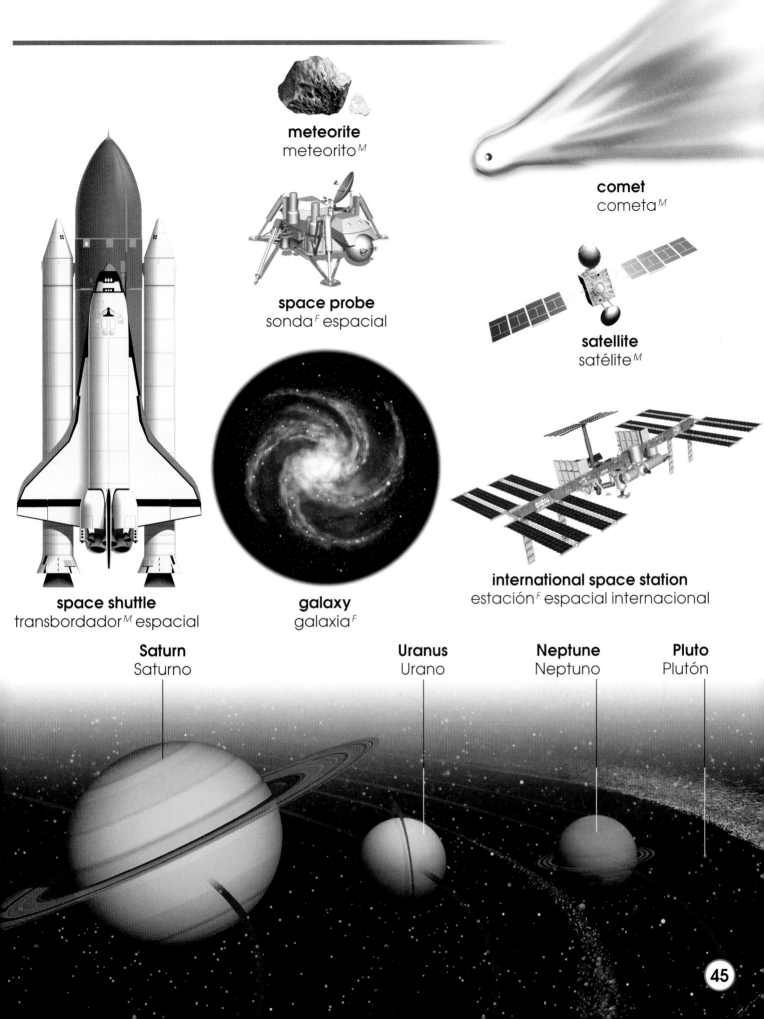

**meteorite**
meteorito[M]

**comet**
cometa[M]

**space probe**
sonda[F] espacial

**satellite**
satélite[M]

**space shuttle**
transbordador[M] espacial

**galaxy**
galaxia[F]

**international space station**
estación[F] espacial internacional

**Saturn**
Saturno

**Uranus**
Urano

**Neptune**
Neptuno

**Pluto**
Plutón

# Earth's landscapes
## Los paisajes de las Tierra

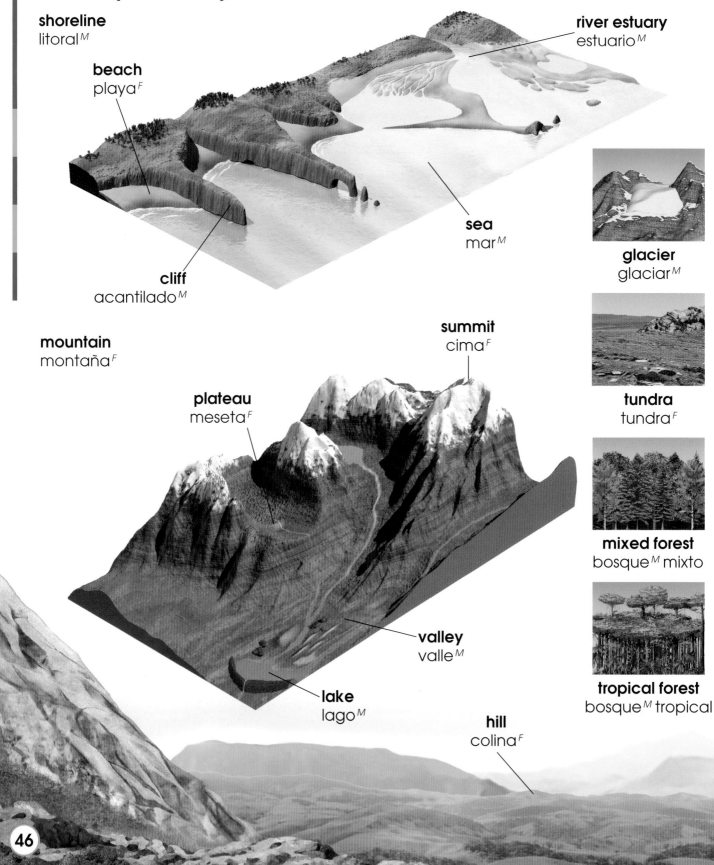

**shoreline**
litoral<sup>M</sup>

**beach**
playa<sup>F</sup>

**river estuary**
estuario<sup>M</sup>

**sea**
mar<sup>M</sup>

**cliff**
acantilado<sup>M</sup>

**mountain**
montaña<sup>F</sup>

**summit**
cima<sup>F</sup>

**plateau**
meseta<sup>F</sup>

**valley**
valle<sup>M</sup>

**lake**
lago<sup>M</sup>

**hill**
colina<sup>F</sup>

**glacier**
glaciar<sup>M</sup>

**tundra**
tundra<sup>F</sup>

**mixed forest**
bosque<sup>M</sup> mixto

**tropical forest**
bosque<sup>M</sup> tropical

# Earth's landscapes
## Los paisajes de las Tierra

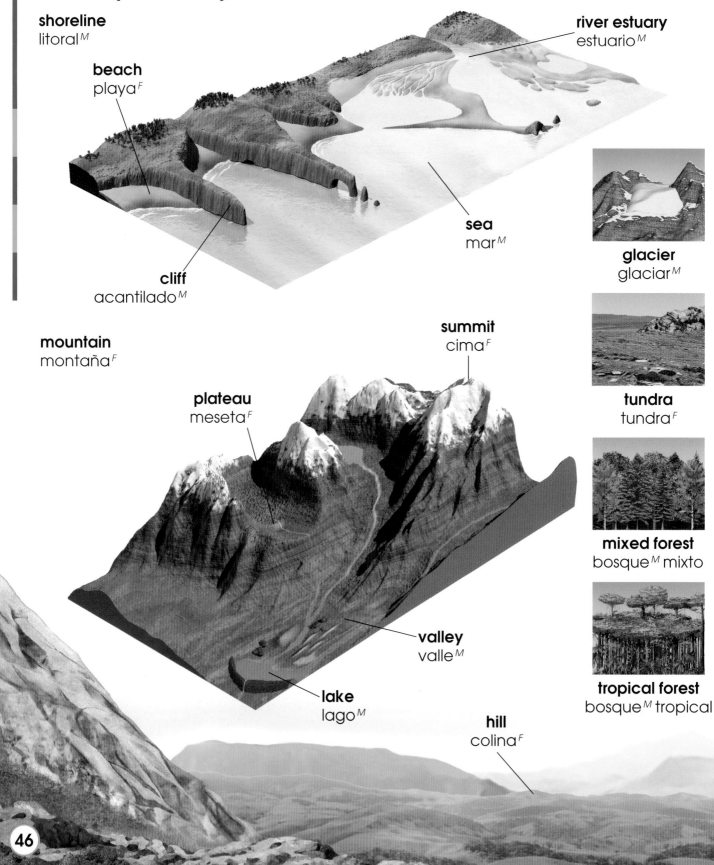

**shoreline** litoral [M]

**beach** playa [F]

**river estuary** estuario [M]

**sea** mar [M]

**cliff** acantilado [M]

**mountain** montaña [F]

**summit** cima [F]

**plateau** meseta [F]

**valley** valle [M]

**lake** lago [M]

**hill** colina [F]

**glacier** glaciar [M]

**tundra** tundra [F]

**mixed forest** bosque [M] mixto

**tropical forest** bosque [M] tropical

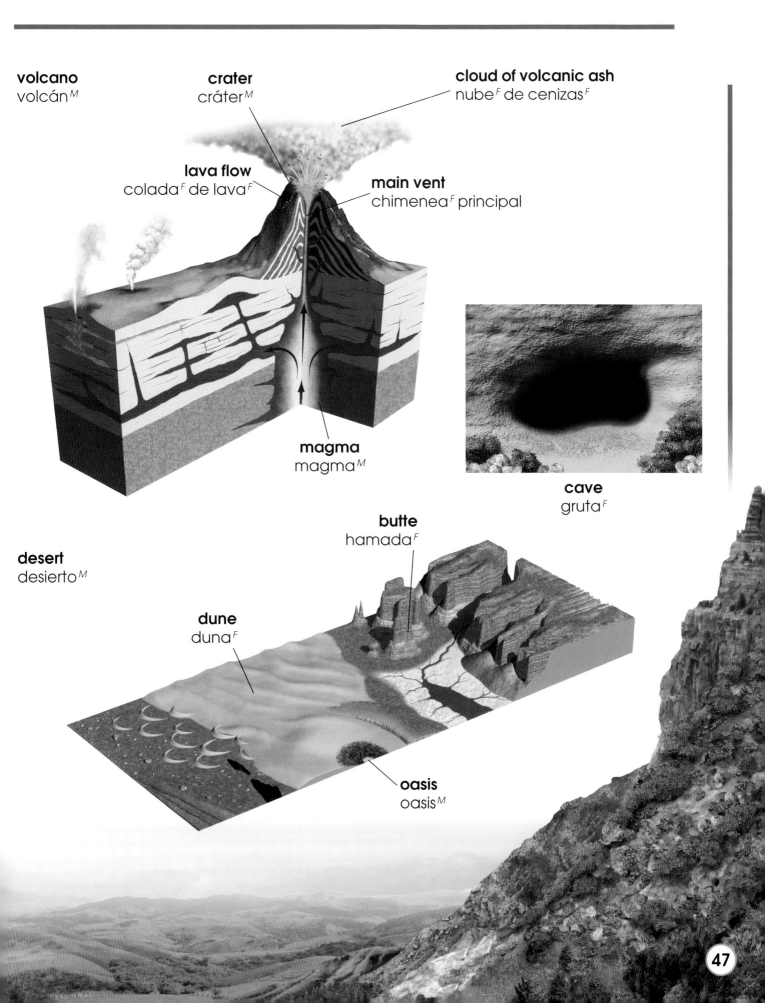

**volcano**
volcán<sup>M</sup>

**crater**
cráter<sup>M</sup>

**cloud of volcanic ash**
nube<sup>F</sup> de cenizas<sup>F</sup>

**lava flow**
colada<sup>F</sup> de lava<sup>F</sup>

**main vent**
chimenea<sup>F</sup> principal

**magma**
magma<sup>M</sup>

**cave**
gruta<sup>F</sup>

**butte**
hamada<sup>F</sup>

**desert**
desierto<sup>M</sup>

**dune**
duna<sup>F</sup>

**oasis**
oasis<sup>M</sup>

# The weather
## El tiempo

rainbow
arco<sup>M</sup> iris

**spring**
primavera<sup>F</sup>

**summer**
verano<sup>M</sup>

**autumn**
otoño<sup>M</sup>

**winter**
invierno<sup>M</sup>

**tropical cyclone**
ciclón<sup>M</sup> tropical

eye
ojo<sup>M</sup>

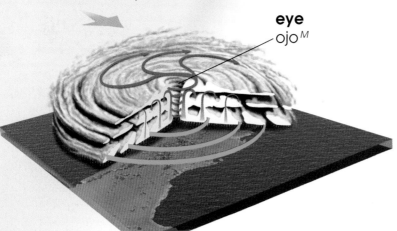

**tornado**
tornado<sup>M</sup>

funnel cloud
nube<sup>F</sup> en forma<sup>F</sup> de embudo<sup>M</sup>

**dew**
rocío<sup>M</sup>

**mist**
neblina<sup>F</sup>

**fog**
niebla<sup>F</sup>

**rime**
escarcha<sup>F</sup>

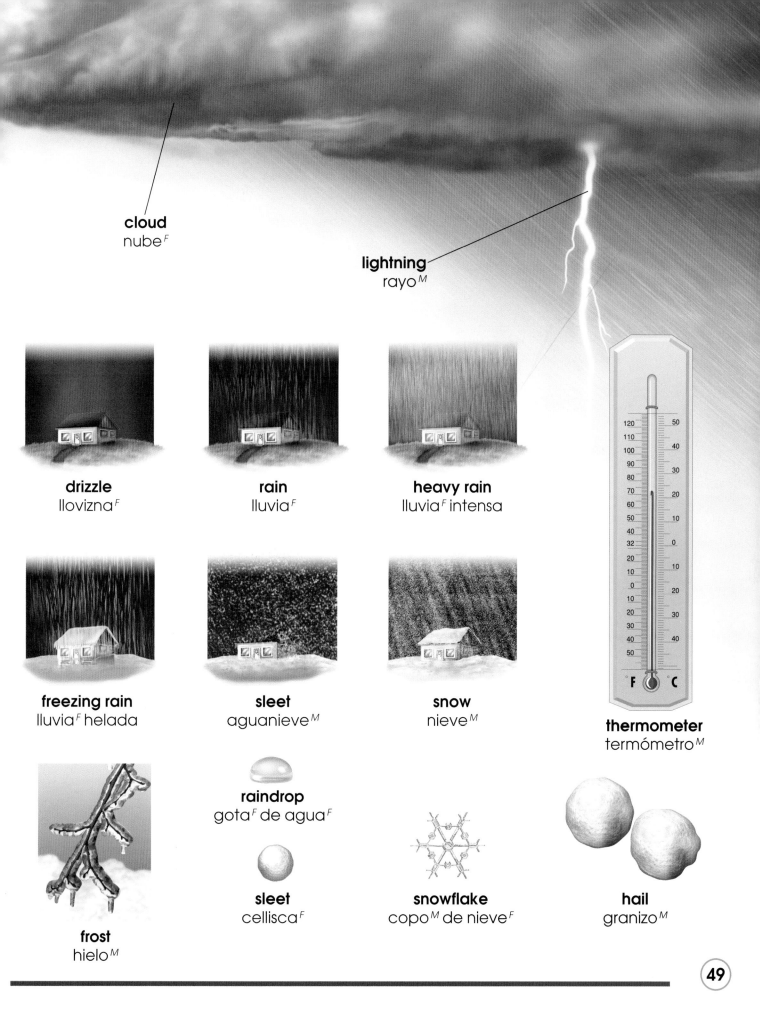

**cloud**
nube<sup>F</sup>

**lightning**
rayo<sup>M</sup>

**drizzle**
llovizna<sup>F</sup>

**rain**
lluvia<sup>F</sup>

**heavy rain**
lluvia<sup>F</sup> intensa

**freezing rain**
lluvia<sup>F</sup> helada

**sleet**
aguanieve<sup>M</sup>

**snow**
nieve<sup>M</sup>

**thermometer**
termómetro<sup>M</sup>

**frost**
hielo<sup>M</sup>

**raindrop**
gota<sup>F</sup> de agua<sup>F</sup>

**sleet**
cellisca<sup>F</sup>

**snowflake**
copo<sup>M</sup> de nieve<sup>F</sup>

**hail**
granizo<sup>M</sup>

# Transportation on water
## Los transportes acuáticos

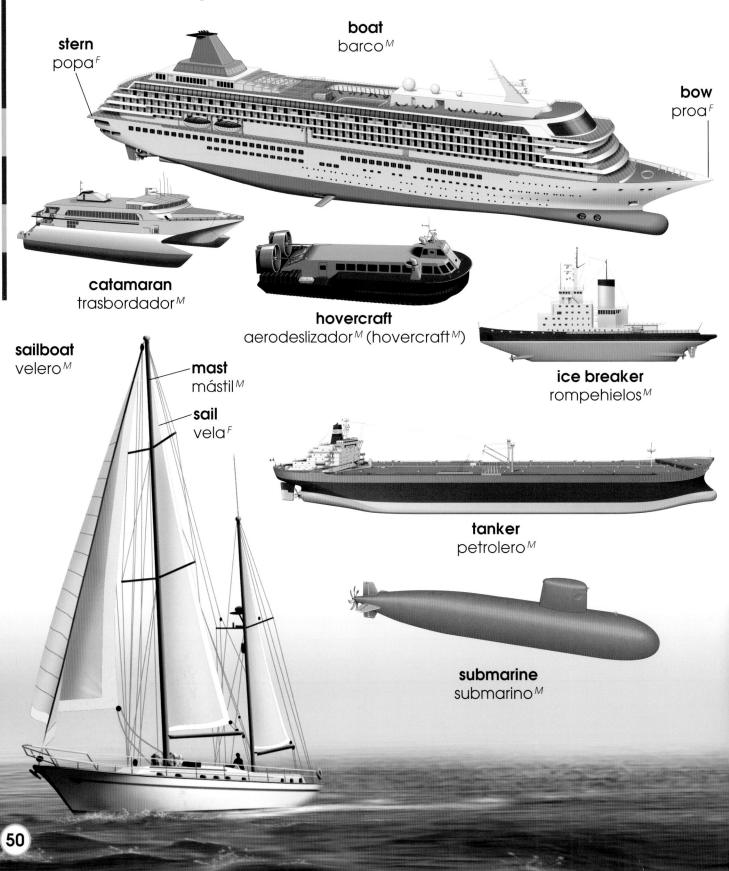

**boat**
barco $^M$

**stern**
popa $^F$

**bow**
proa $^F$

**catamaran**
trasbordador $^M$

**hovercraft**
aerodeslizador $^M$ (hovercraft $^M$)

**ice breaker**
rompehielos $^M$

**sailboat**
velero $^M$

**mast**
mástil $^M$

**sail**
vela $^F$

**tanker**
petrolero $^M$

**submarine**
submarino $^M$

**anchor**
ancla<sup>F</sup>

**life buoy**
salvavidas<sup>M</sup>

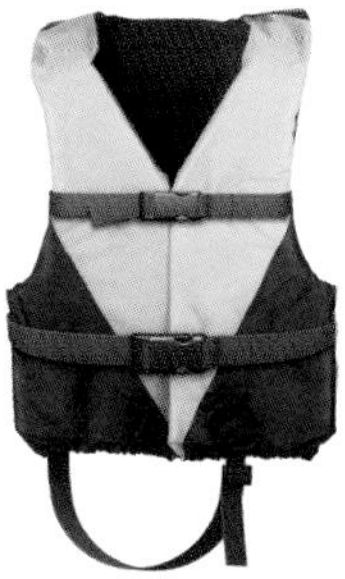

**personal flotation device**
chaleco<sup>M</sup> salvavidas

**personal watercraft**
moto<sup>F</sup> acuática

**paddle**
pala<sup>F</sup>

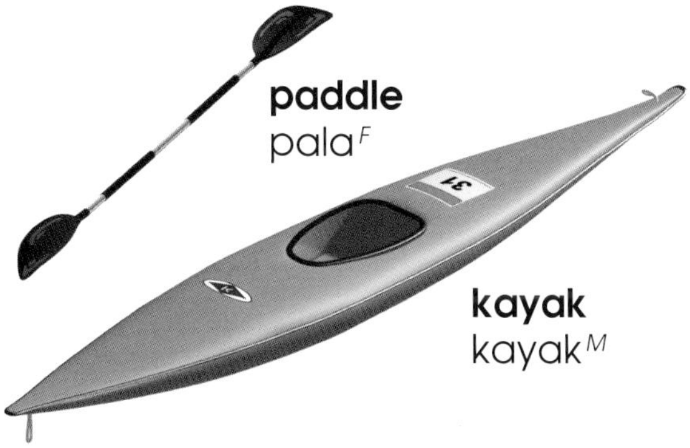

**kayak**
kayak<sup>M</sup>

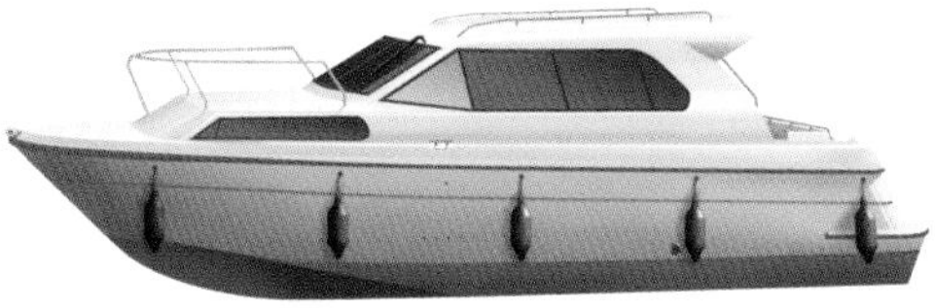

**yacht**
yate<sup>M</sup>

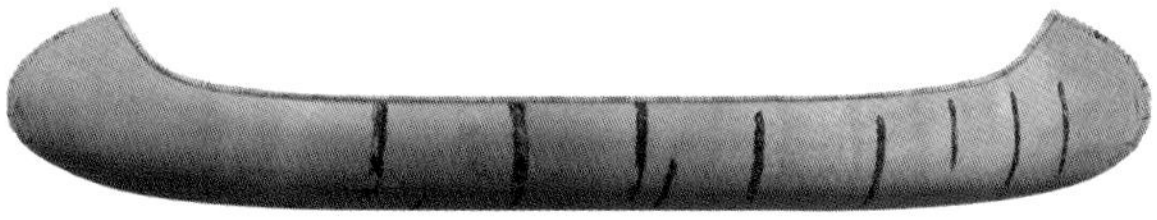

**lighthouse**
faro<sup>M</sup> marítimo

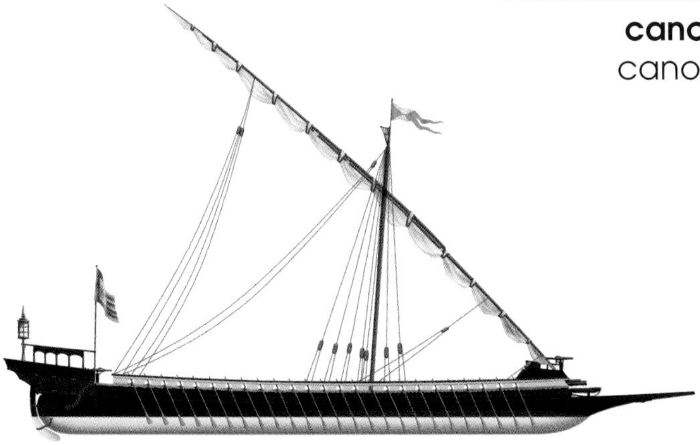

**canoe**
canoa<sup>F</sup>

**galley**
galera<sup>F</sup>

**caravel**
carabela<sup>F</sup>

**container ship**
carguero<sup>M</sup> portacontenedores

**speedboat**
lancha<sup>F</sup> pequeña

# Transportation in the air
## Los transportes aéreos

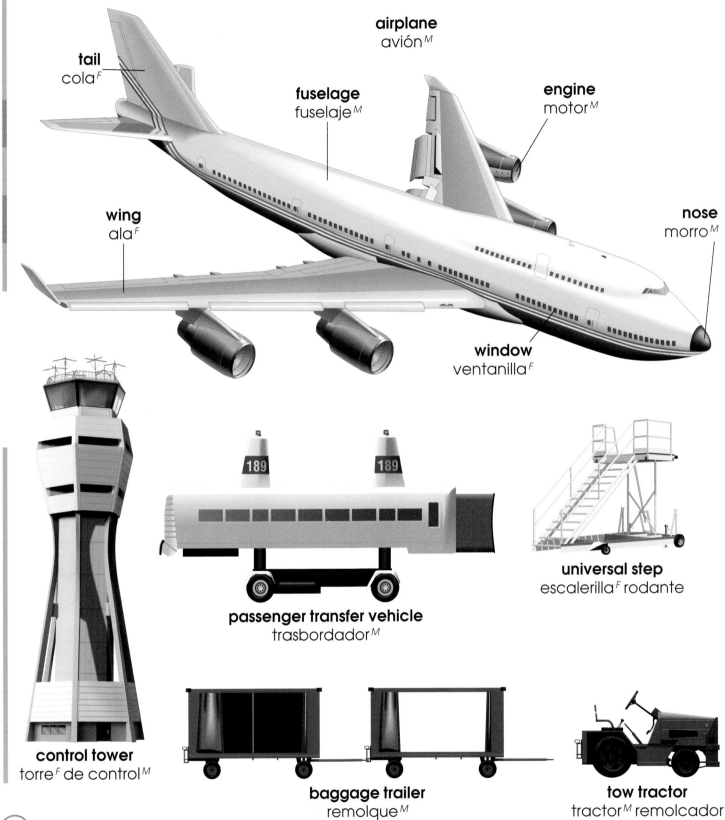

**airplane**
avión$^M$

**tail**
cola$^F$

**fuselage**
fuselaje$^M$

**engine**
motor$^M$

**nose**
morro$^M$

**wing**
ala$^F$

**window**
ventanilla$^F$

**control tower**
torre$^F$ de control$^M$

**passenger transfer vehicle**
trasbordador$^M$

189

189

**universal step**
escalerilla$^F$ rodante

**baggage trailer**
remolque$^M$

**tow tractor**
tractor$^M$ remolcador

**seaplane**
hidroavión$^M$

**fire-fighting aircraft**
avión$^M$ cisterna$^F$

**business aircraft**
avión$^M$ particular

**cargo aircraft**
avión$^M$ de carga

**basket**
barquilla$^F$

**hot-air balloon**
globo$^M$ aerostático

**biplane**
biplano$^M$

**light aircraft**
avión$^M$ ligero

**helicopter**
helicóptero$^M$

# Transportation on land
## Los transportes terrestres

**child carrier**
silla<sup>F</sup> porta-niño<sup>M</sup>

**bicycle helmet**
casco<sup>M</sup> de bicicleta<sup>F</sup>

**bicycle**
bicicleta<sup>F</sup>

**pedal**
pedal<sup>M</sup>

**brake**
freno<sup>M</sup>

**seat**
sillín<sup>M</sup>

**handlebars**
manillar<sup>M</sup>

**drive chain**
cadena<sup>F</sup> de transmisión<sup>F</sup>

**motorcycle helmet**
casco<sup>M</sup> de moto<sup>F</sup>

**motorcycle**
motocicleta<sup>F</sup>

**motor scooter**
escúter<sup>M</sup>

**child safety seat**
silla<sup>F</sup> de seguridad<sup>F</sup> para niños<sup>M</sup>

**highway crossing**
paso<sup>M</sup> a nivel<sup>M</sup>

**railroad track**
vía<sup>F</sup> férrea

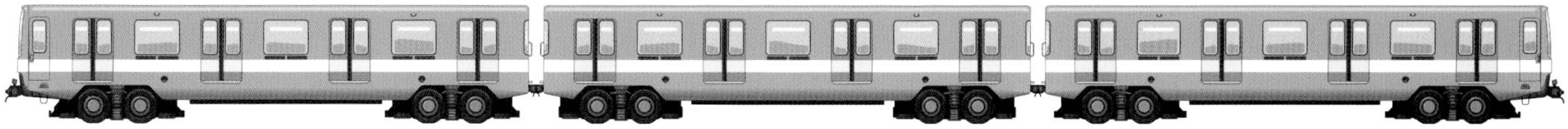

**subway train**
tren[M] subterráneo

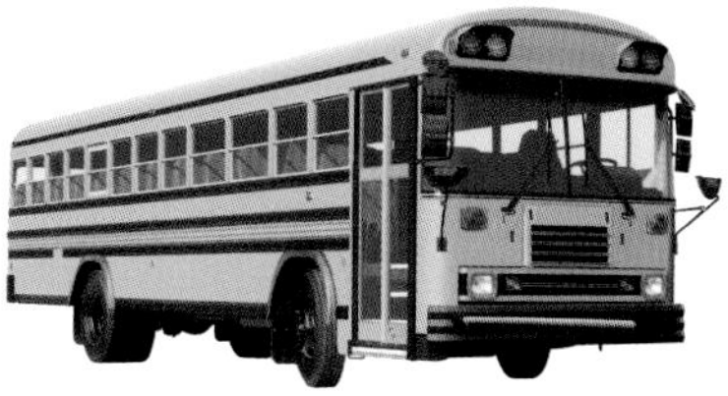

**school bus**
autobús[M] escolar

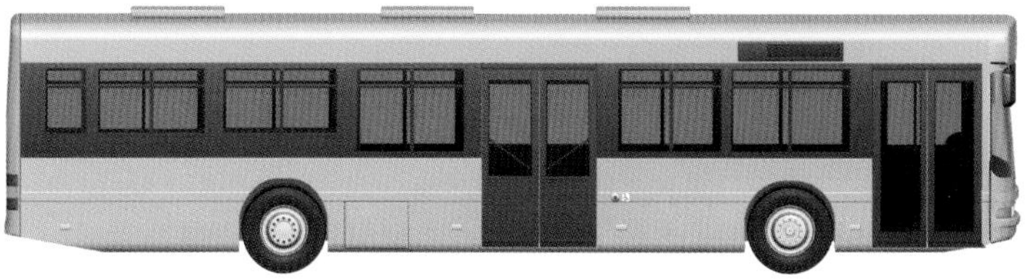

**city bus**
autobús[M] urbano

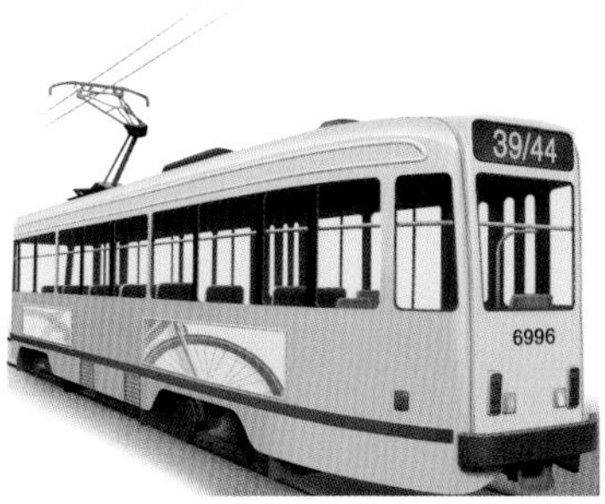
39/44
6996

**streetcar**
tranvía[F]

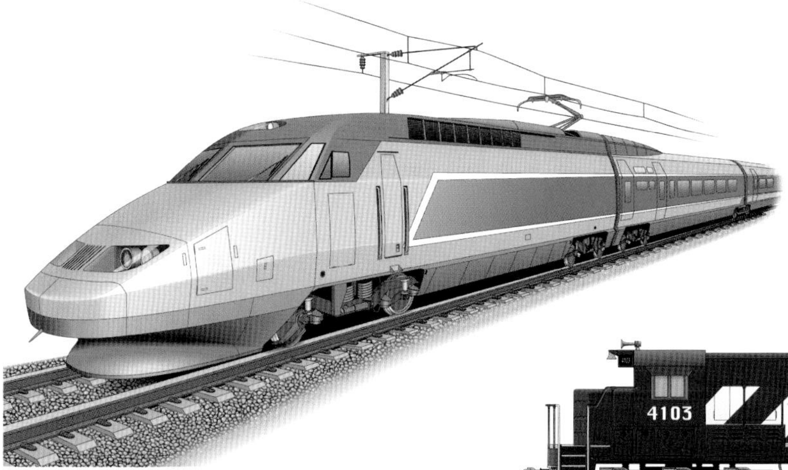

**train**
tren[M]

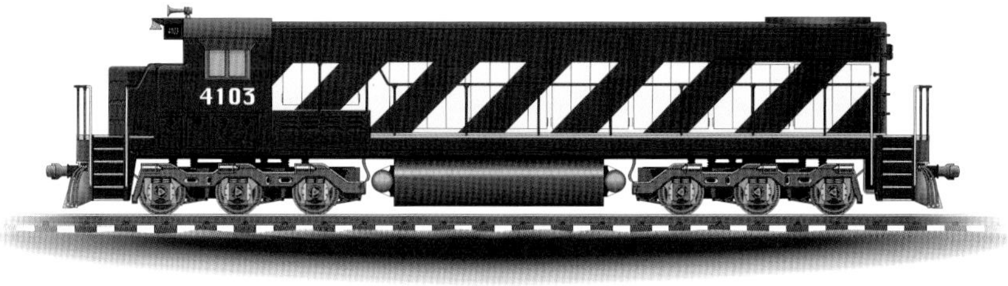
4103

**locomotive**
locomotora[F]

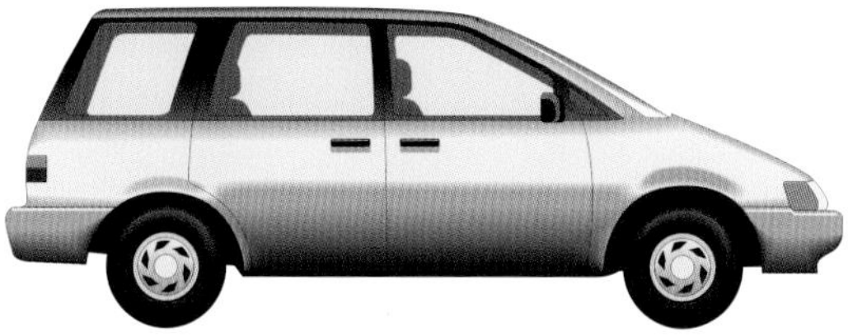

**minivan**
monovolumen[M]

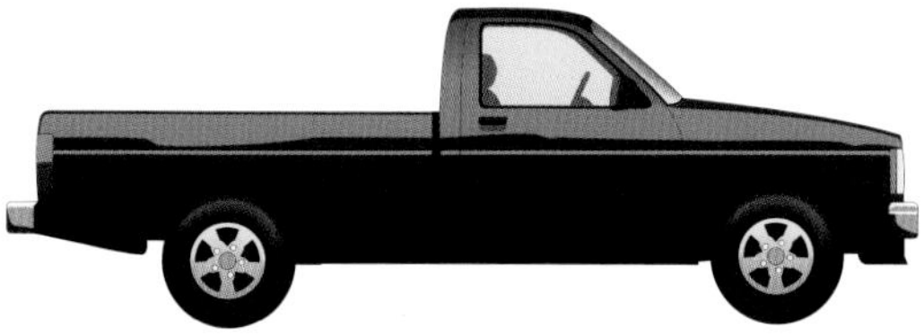

**pickup truck**
camioneta[F]

**car**
carro[M]

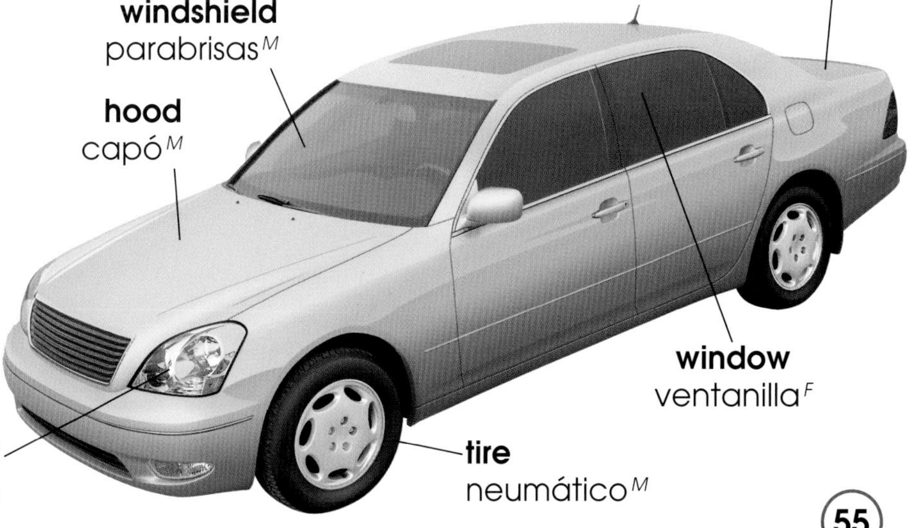
**trunk**
maletero[M]
**windshield**
parabrisas[M]
**hood**
capó[M]
**window**
ventanilla[F]
**headlight**
faro[M] delantero
**tire**
neumático[M]

# The city
## La ciudad

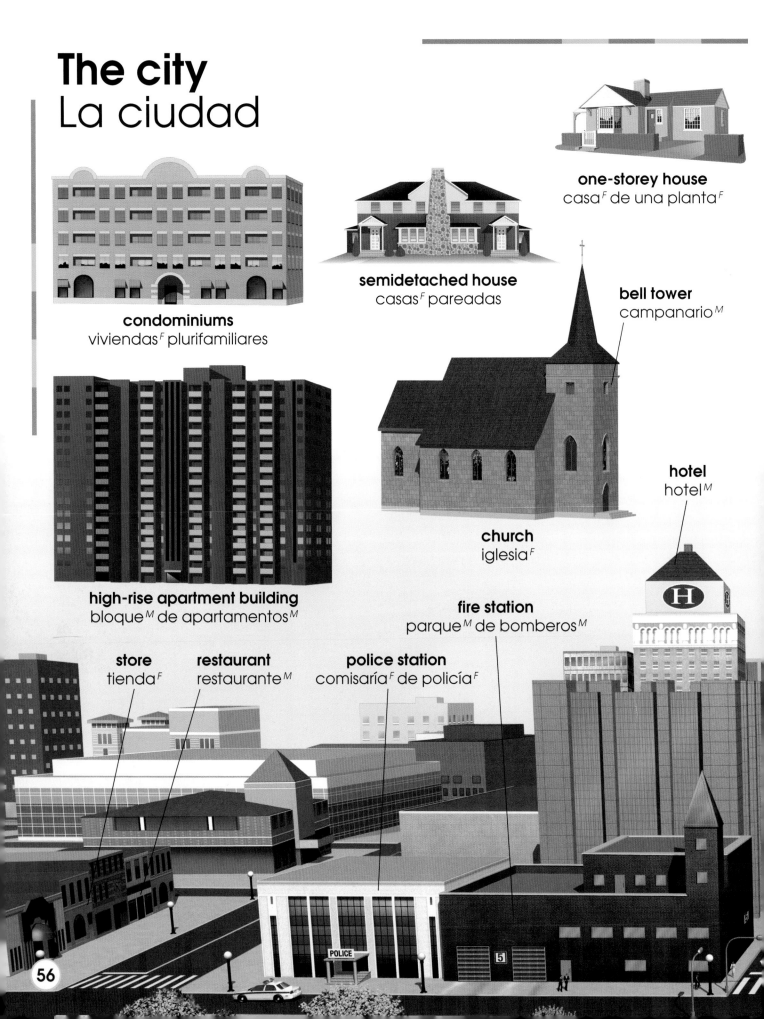

one-storey house
casa$^F$ de una planta$^F$

condominiums
viviendas$^F$ plurifamiliares

semidetached house
casas$^F$ pareadas

bell tower
campanario$^M$

hotel
hotel$^M$

church
iglesia$^F$

high-rise apartment building
bloque$^M$ de apartamentos$^M$

fire station
parque$^M$ de bomberos$^M$

store
tienda$^F$

restaurant
restaurante$^M$

police station
comisaría$^F$ de policía$^F$

POLICE

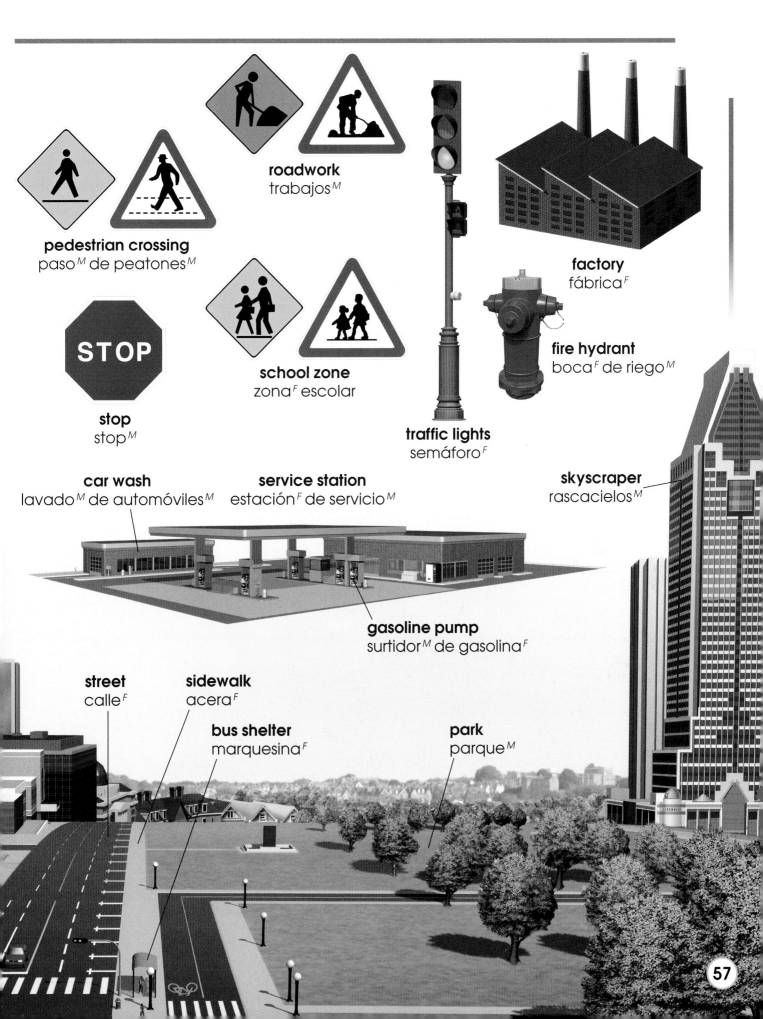

**pedestrian crossing**
paso<sup>M</sup> de peatones<sup>M</sup>

**roadwork**
trabajos<sup>M</sup>

**stop**
stop<sup>M</sup>

**school zone**
zona<sup>F</sup> escolar

**factory**
fábrica<sup>F</sup>

**fire hydrant**
boca<sup>F</sup> de riego<sup>M</sup>

**traffic lights**
semáforo<sup>F</sup>

**car wash**
lavado<sup>M</sup> de automóviles<sup>M</sup>

**service station**
estación<sup>F</sup> de servicio<sup>M</sup>

**skyscraper**
rascacielos<sup>M</sup>

**gasoline pump**
surtidor<sup>M</sup> de gasolina<sup>F</sup>

**street**
calle<sup>F</sup>

**sidewalk**
acera<sup>F</sup>

**bus shelter**
marquesina<sup>F</sup>

**park**
parque<sup>M</sup>

# Trades
## Los oficios

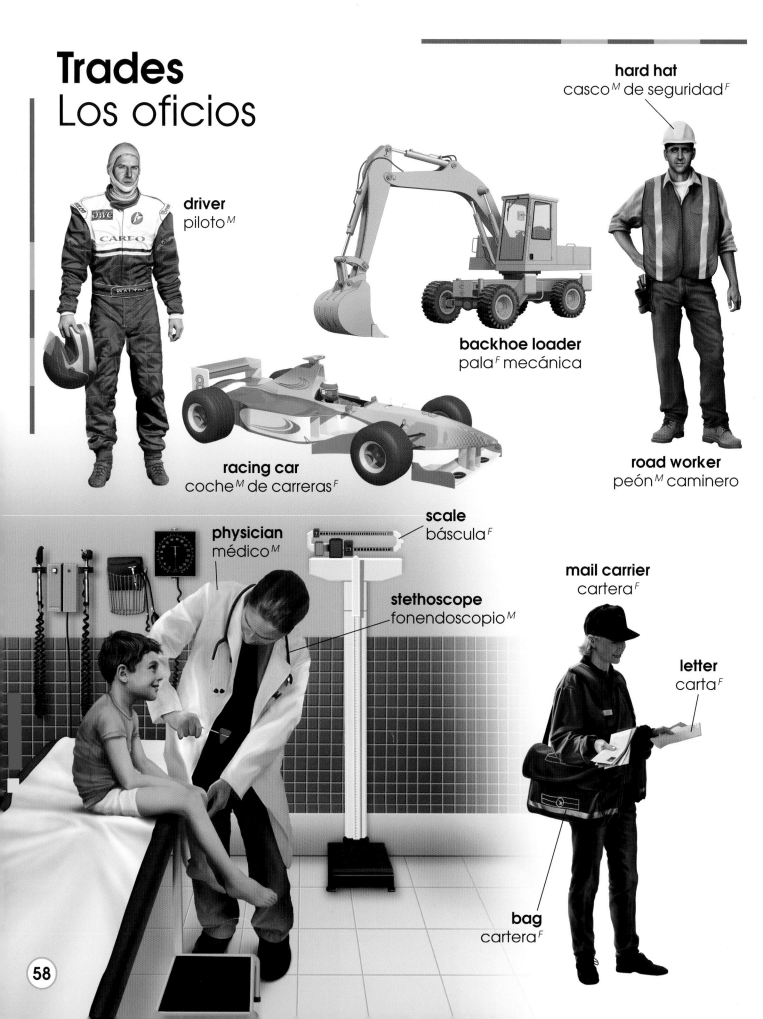

**driver**
piloto$^M$

**backhoe loader**
pala$^F$ mecánica

**hard hat**
casco$^M$ de seguridad$^F$

**racing car**
coche$^M$ de carreras$^F$

**road worker**
peón$^M$ caminero

**scale**
báscula$^F$

**physician**
médico$^M$

**stethoscope**
fonendoscopio$^M$

**mail carrier**
cartera$^F$

**letter**
carta$^F$

**bag**
cartera$^F$

**firefighter**
bombero<sup>M</sup>

**mask**
máscara<sup>M</sup>

**helmet**
casco<sup>M</sup>

**compressed-air cylinder**
bombona<sup>F</sup> de aire<sup>M</sup> comprimido

**hatchet**
hacha<sup>F</sup>

**fire extinguisher**
extintor<sup>M</sup>

**fire hose**
manguera<sup>F</sup> de incendios<sup>M</sup>

**fire truck**
camión<sup>M</sup> de bomberos<sup>M</sup>

**duty belt**
cinturón<sup>M</sup> de servicio<sup>M</sup>

**police car**
coche<sup>M</sup> de policía<sup>F</sup>

**police officer**
agente<sup>M</sup> de policía<sup>F</sup>

**astronaut**
astronauta<sup>M</sup>

# School
## El colegio

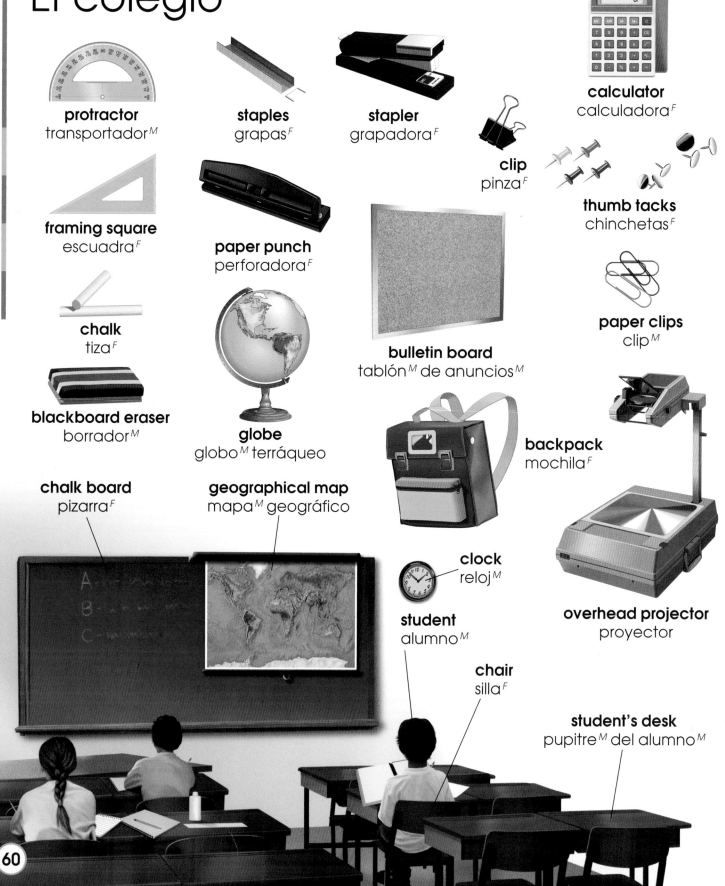

**protractor**
transportador$^M$

**staples**
grapas$^F$

**stapler**
grapadora$^F$

**calculator**
calculadora$^F$

**framing square**
escuadra$^F$

**paper punch**
perforadora$^F$

**clip**
pinza$^F$

**thumb tacks**
chinchetas$^F$

**chalk**
tiza$^F$

**bulletin board**
tablón$^M$ de anuncios$^M$

**paper clips**
clip$^M$

**blackboard eraser**
borrador$^M$

**globe**
globo$^M$ terráqueo

**chalk board**
pizarra$^F$

**geographical map**
mapa$^M$ geográfico

**backpack**
mochila$^F$

**clock**
reloj$^M$

**student**
alumno$^M$

**chair**
silla$^F$

**overhead projector**
proyector

**student's desk**
pupitre$^M$ del alumno$^M$

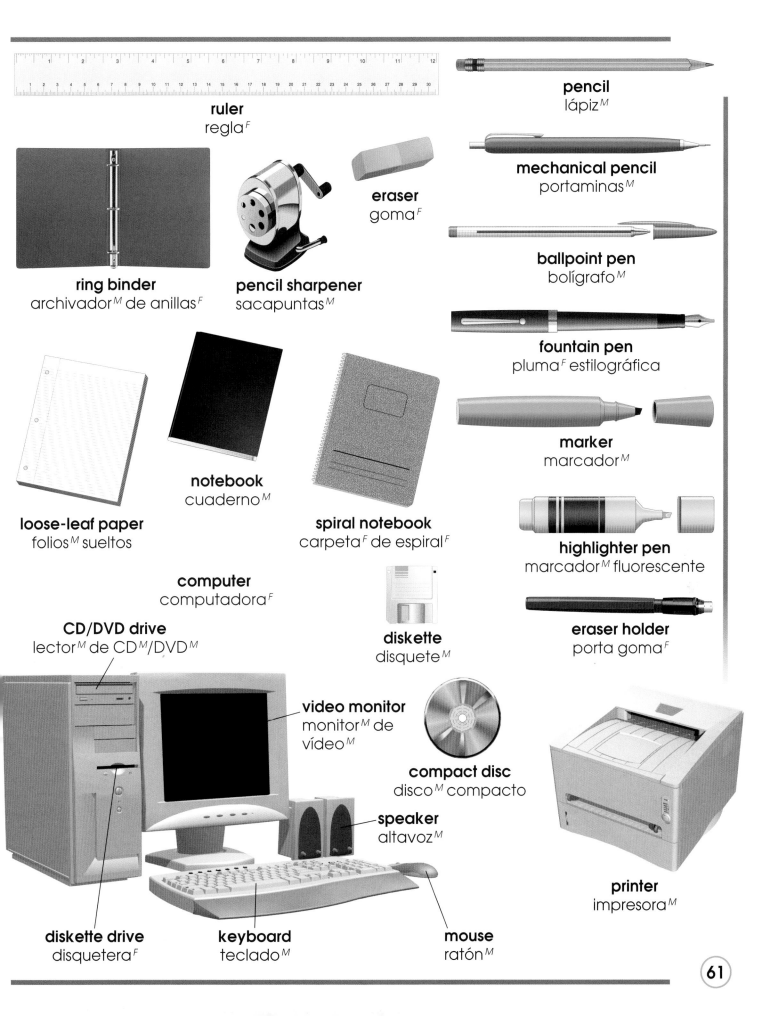

**ruler**
regla^F

**pencil**
lápiz^M

**mechanical pencil**
portaminas^M

**eraser**
goma^F

**ballpoint pen**
bolígrafo^M

**ring binder**
archivador^M de anillas^F

**pencil sharpener**
sacapuntas^M

**fountain pen**
pluma^F estilográfica

**marker**
marcador^M

**notebook**
cuaderno^M

**spiral notebook**
carpeta^F de espiral^F

**highlighter pen**
marcador^M fluorescente

**loose-leaf paper**
folios^M sueltos

**computer**
computadora^F

**diskette**
disquete^M

**eraser holder**
porta goma^F

**CD/DVD drive**
lector^M de CD^M/DVD^M

**video monitor**
monitor^M de
vídeo^M

**compact disc**
disco^M compacto

**speaker**
altavoz^M

**printer**
impresora^M

**diskette drive**
disquetera^F

**keyboard**
teclado^M

**mouse**
ratón^M

# Colors and shapes
## Los colores y las formas

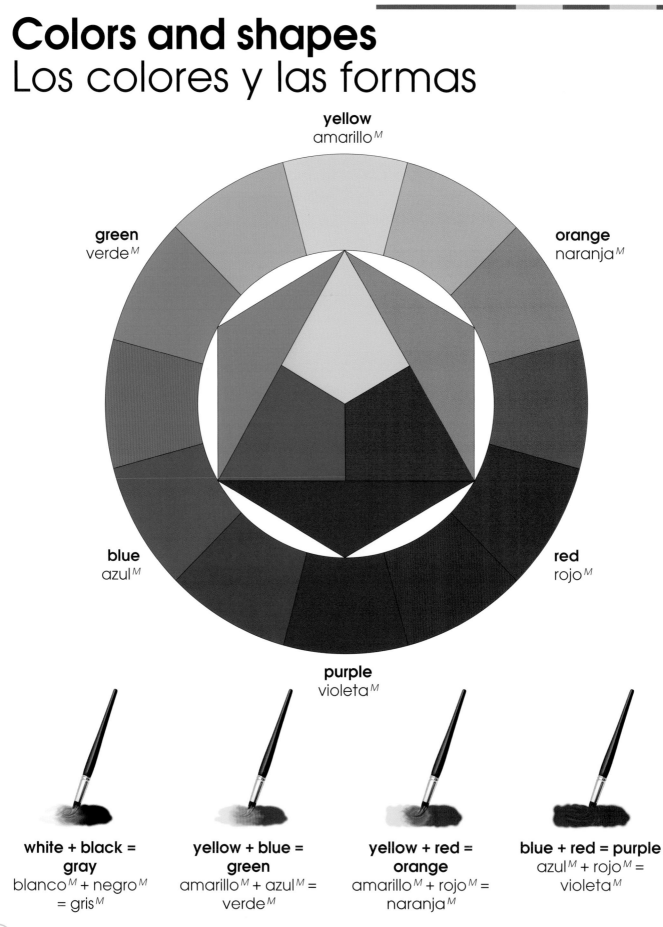

yellow
amarillo $^M$

green
verde $^M$

orange
naranja $^M$

blue
azul $^M$

red
rojo $^M$

purple
violeta $^M$

**white + black = gray**
blanco $^M$ + negro $^M$ = gris $^M$

**yellow + blue = green**
amarillo $^M$ + azul $^M$ = verde $^M$

**yellow + red = orange**
amarillo $^M$ + rojo $^M$ = naranja $^M$

**blue + red = purple**
azul $^M$ + rojo $^M$ = violeta $^M$

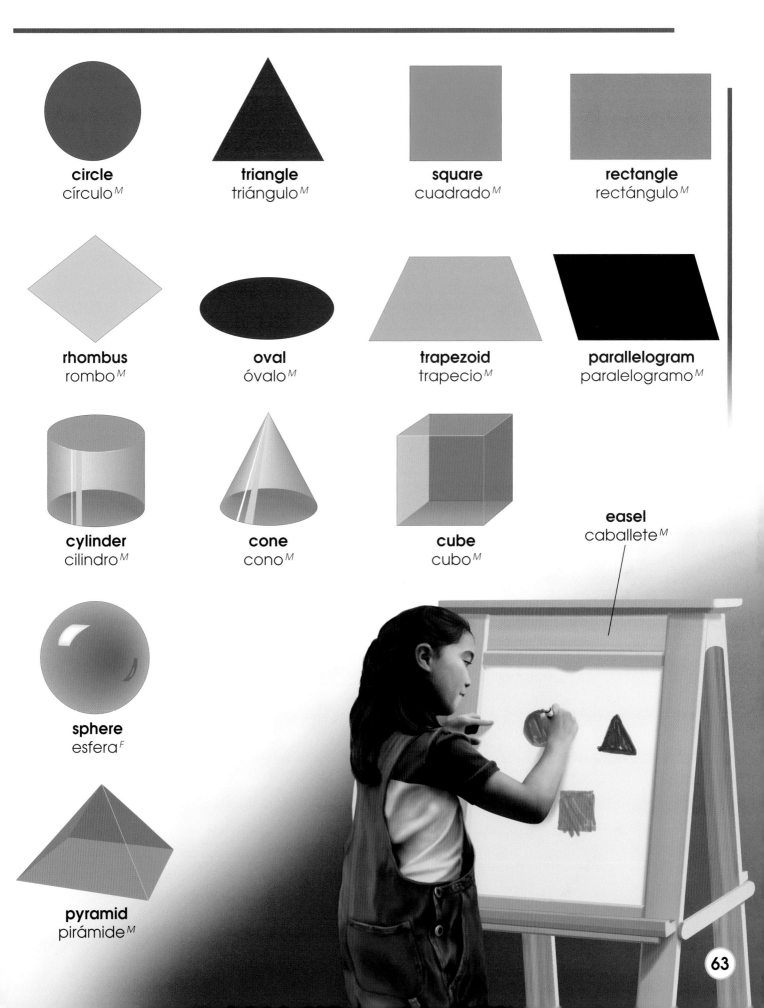

**circle**
círculo<sup>M</sup>

**triangle**
triángulo<sup>M</sup>

**square**
cuadrado<sup>M</sup>

**rectangle**
rectángulo<sup>M</sup>

**rhombus**
rombo<sup>M</sup>

**oval**
óvalo<sup>M</sup>

**trapezoid**
trapecio<sup>M</sup>

**parallelogram**
paralelogramo<sup>M</sup>

**cylinder**
cilindro<sup>M</sup>

**cone**
cono<sup>M</sup>

**cube**
cubo<sup>M</sup>

**easel**
caballete<sup>M</sup>

**sphere**
esfera<sup>F</sup>

**pyramid**
pirámide<sup>M</sup>

# Numbers and letters
## Los números y las letras

**one**
uno<sup>M</sup>

**two**
dos<sup>M</sup>

**three**
tres<sup>M</sup>

**four**
cuatro<sup>M</sup>

**five**
cinco<sup>M</sup>

**six**
seis<sup>M</sup>

**seven**
siete<sup>M</sup>

**eight**
ocho<sup>M</sup>

**nine**
nueve<sup>M</sup>

**ten**
diez<sup>M</sup>

**+**
**plus**
suma<sup>F</sup>

**—**
**minus**
resta<sup>F</sup>

**÷**
**divided by**
división<sup>F</sup>

**X**
**multiplied by**
multiplicación<sup>F</sup>

**=**
**equals**
igual a

## alphabet
alfabeto <sup>M</sup>

# Aa Bb Cc Dd Ee
# Ff Gg Hh Ii Jj Kk
# Ll Mm Nn Oo Pp
# Qq Rr Ss Tt Uu Vv
# Ww Xx Yy Zz

abacus
ábaco <sup>M</sup>

# Music
## La música

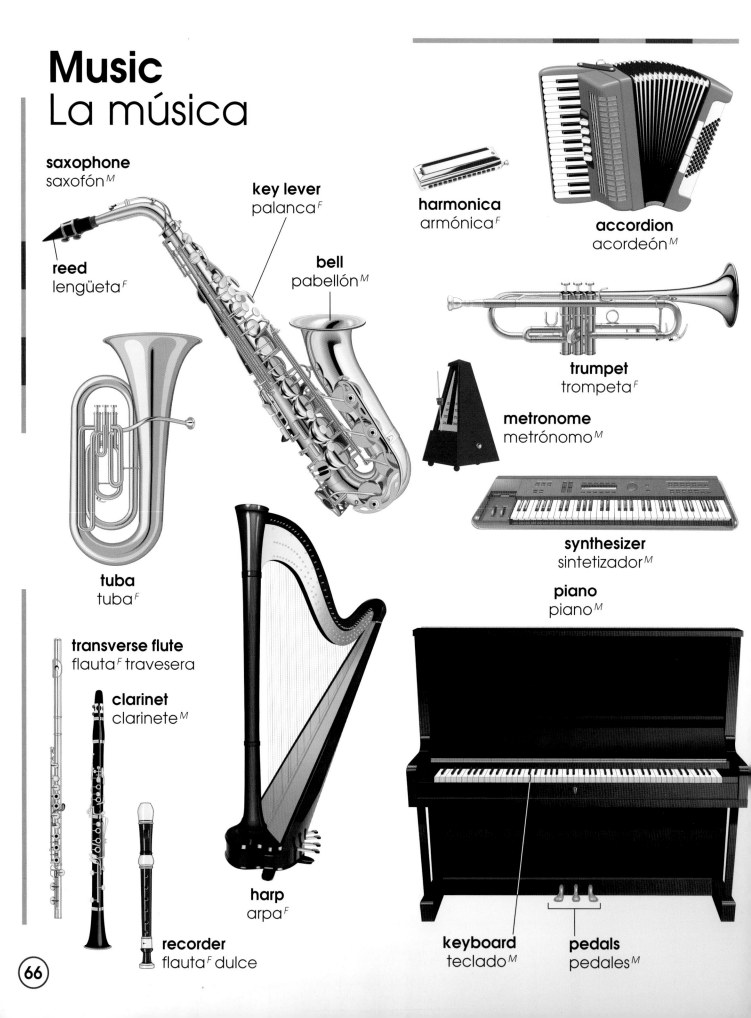

**saxophone**
saxofón$^M$

**key lever**
palanca$^F$

**reed**
lengüeta$^F$

**bell**
pabellón$^M$

**harmonica**
armónica$^F$

**accordion**
acordeón$^M$

**trumpet**
trompeta$^F$

**metronome**
metrónomo$^M$

**synthesizer**
sintetizador$^M$

**piano**
piano$^M$

**tuba**
tuba$^F$

**transverse flute**
flauta$^F$ travesera

**clarinet**
clarinete$^M$

**harp**
arpa$^F$

**recorder**
flauta$^F$ dulce

**keyboard**
teclado$^M$

**pedals**
pedales$^M$

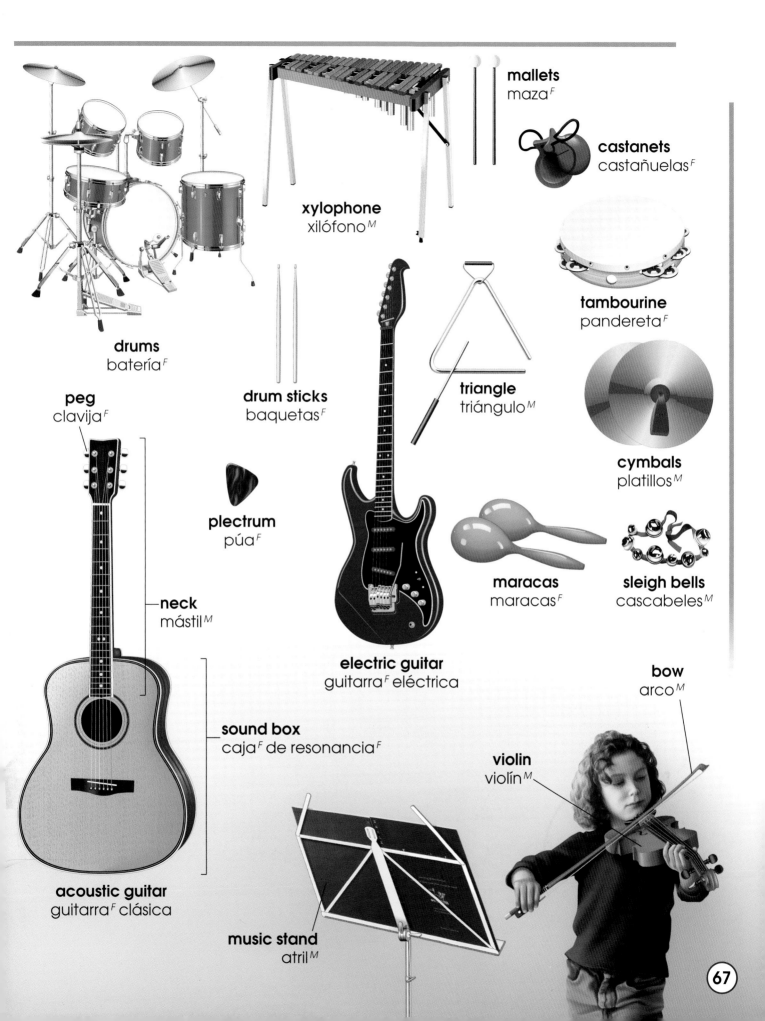

**mallets**
maza<sup>F</sup>

**castanets**
castañuelas<sup>F</sup>

**xylophone**
xilófono<sup>M</sup>

**tambourine**
pandereta<sup>F</sup>

**drums**
batería<sup>F</sup>

**triangle**
triángulo<sup>M</sup>

**drum sticks**
baquetas<sup>F</sup>

**peg**
clavija<sup>F</sup>

**cymbals**
platillos<sup>M</sup>

**plectrum**
púa<sup>F</sup>

**neck**
mástil<sup>M</sup>

**maracas**
maracas<sup>F</sup>

**sleigh bells**
cascabeles<sup>M</sup>

**electric guitar**
guitarra<sup>F</sup> eléctrica

**bow**
arco<sup>M</sup>

**sound box**
caja<sup>F</sup> de resonancia<sup>F</sup>

**violin**
violín<sup>M</sup>

**acoustic guitar**
guitarra<sup>F</sup> clásica

**music stand**
atril<sup>M</sup>

# Sports
## Los deportes

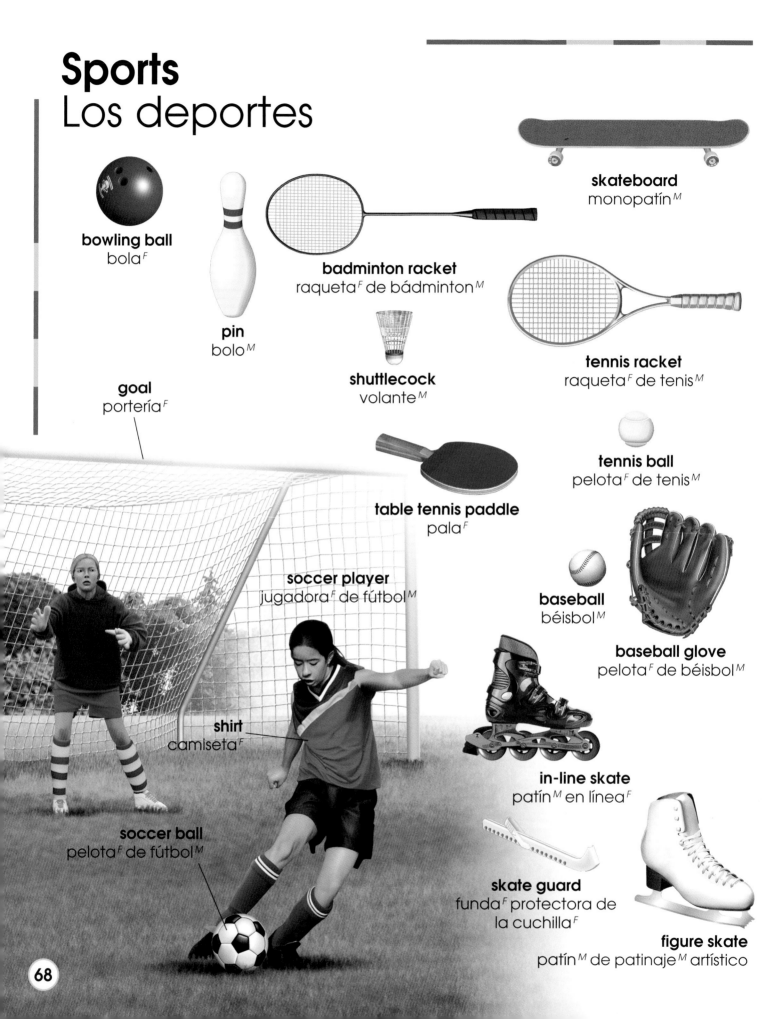

**bowling ball**
bola<sup>F</sup>

**pin**
bolo<sup>M</sup>

**badminton racket**
raqueta<sup>F</sup> de bádminton<sup>M</sup>

**shuttlecock**
volante<sup>M</sup>

**skateboard**
monopatín<sup>M</sup>

**tennis racket**
raqueta<sup>F</sup> de tenis<sup>M</sup>

**tennis ball**
pelota<sup>F</sup> de tenis<sup>M</sup>

**table tennis paddle**
pala<sup>F</sup>

**goal**
portería<sup>F</sup>

**soccer player**
jugadora<sup>F</sup> de fútbol<sup>M</sup>

**baseball**
béisbol<sup>M</sup>

**baseball glove**
pelota<sup>F</sup> de béisbol<sup>M</sup>

**shirt**
camiseta<sup>F</sup>

**in-line skate**
patín<sup>M</sup> en línea<sup>F</sup>

**soccer ball**
pelota<sup>F</sup> de fútbol<sup>M</sup>

**skate guard**
funda<sup>F</sup> protectora de
la cuchilla<sup>F</sup>

**figure skate**
patín<sup>M</sup> de patinaje<sup>M</sup> artístico

**snowboard**
tabla$^F$ de snowboard$^M$

**cross-country skier**
fondista$^M$

**basketball**
balón$^M$ de baloncesto$^M$

**basket**
canasta$^F$

**alpine skier**
esquiador$^M$ alpino

**hockey player**
jugadora$^F$ de fútbol$^M$

**helmet**
casco$^M$

**karateka**
karateka$^M$

**swimmer**
nadador$^M$

**stick**
palo$^M$

**football player**
jugador$^M$ de fútbol$^M$
americano

**sprinter**
velocista$^F$

**football**
balón$^M$ de fútbol$^M$
americano

**golf ball**
pelota$^F$ de golf$^M$

**golf club**
palo$^M$ de golf$^M$

**trampoline**
trampolín$^M$

69

# Camping
## El camping

**Swiss Army knife**
navaja<sup>F</sup> multiusos suiza

**air mattress**
colchoneta<sup>F</sup> de aire<sup>M</sup>

**sleeping bag**
saco<sup>F</sup> de dormir

**foam pad**
colchoneta<sup>F</sup> de espuma<sup>F</sup>

**matchbox**
caja<sup>F</sup> de cerillas<sup>F</sup>

**cutlery set**
cubertería<sup>F</sup>

**inflator**
inflador<sup>M</sup>

**cup**
taza<sup>F</sup>

**vacuum bottle**
termo<sup>M</sup>

**camp stove**
hornillo<sup>M</sup>

**frying pan**
sartén<sup>F</sup>

**plate**
plato<sup>M</sup>

**campfire**
hoguera<sup>F</sup>

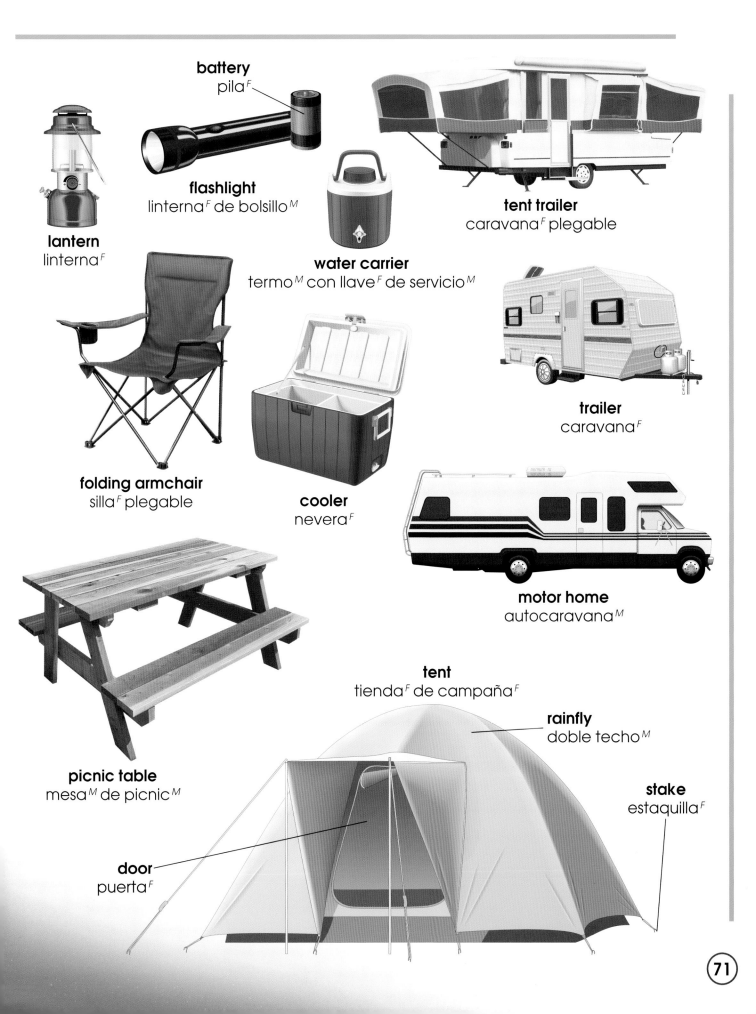

**battery**
pila$^F$

**flashlight**
linterna$^F$ de bolsillo$^M$

**lantern**
linterna$^F$

**water carrier**
termo$^M$ con llave$^F$ de servicio$^M$

**tent trailer**
caravana$^F$ plegable

**folding armchair**
silla$^F$ plegable

**cooler**
nevera$^F$

**trailer**
caravana$^F$

**motor home**
autocaravana$^M$

**picnic table**
mesa$^M$ de picnic$^M$

**tent**
tienda$^F$ de campaña$^F$

**rainfly**
doble techo$^M$

**stake**
estaquilla$^F$

**door**
puerta$^F$

# Parties and holidays
## Las fiestas

confetti
confeti<sup>M</sup>

streamers
serpentinas<sup>F</sup>

crackers
petardos<sup>M</sup>

candle
vela<sup>F</sup>

birthday cake
tarta<sup>F</sup> de cumpleaños<sup>M</sup>

gift wrap
papel<sup>M</sup> de regalo<sup>M</sup>

balloon
globo<sup>M</sup>

paper streamer
guirnalda<sup>F</sup> de papel<sup>M</sup>

flute
silbato<sup>M</sup>

hat
sombrero<sup>M</sup>

greeting card
tarjeta<sup>F</sup> de felicitación<sup>F</sup>

loot bag
bolsa<sup>F</sup> de sorpresas<sup>F</sup>

**fireworks**
fuegos<sup>M</sup> artificiales

**headdress**
cofia<sup>F</sup> cónica

**mask**
careta<sup>F</sup>

**star**
estrella<sup>F</sup>

**Easter eggs**
huevos<sup>V</sup> de Pascua<sup>F</sup>

**ribbon**
cinta<sup>F</sup>

**garland**
espumillón<sup>M</sup>

**gift**
regalo<sup>M</sup>

**piñata**
piñata<sup>F</sup>

**ball**
bola<sup>F</sup>

**gift bag**
bolsa<sup>F</sup> regalo<sup>M</sup>

**Halloween pumpkin**
calabaza<sup>F</sup> de Halloween<sup>M</sup>

**Christmas tree**
árbol<sup>M</sup> de Navidad<sup>M</sup>

# Costumes and characters
## Los disfraces y los personajes

**magician**
mago$^M$

**juggler**
juglar$^M$

**monster**
monstruo$^M$

**princess**
princesa$^F$

**king**
rey$^M$

**gnome**
gnomo$^M$

**robot**
robot$^M$

**witch**
bruja$^F$

**fairy**
hada$^F$

**sleigh**
trineo$^M$

**Santa Claus**
papá$^M$ Noel/Santa Claus

**reindeer**
reno$^M$

**ghost**
fantasma$^M$

**knight**
caballero<sup>M</sup>

**Gallic warrior**
guerrero<sup>M</sup> galo

**soldier**
soldado<sup>M</sup>

**Roman legionary**
legionario<sup>M</sup> romano

**pirate**
pirata<sup>M</sup>

**trainer**
domador<sup>M</sup>

**cowboy**
vaquero<sup>M</sup>

**Native American**
indio<sup>M</sup> americano

**ballerina**
bailarina<sup>F</sup>

**clown**
payaso<sup>M</sup>

**dragon**
dragón<sup>M</sup>

# English Index

## A

abacus 65
abdomen 4
above-ground swimming pool 11
accordion 66
acoustic guitar 67
adhesive bandage 14
adhesive tape 19
afraid 7
air mattress 70
airplane 52
alarm clock 12
alfalfa sprouts 25
alga 38
allosaurus 40
alphabet 65
alpine skier 69
aluminum foil 28
anchor 51
angry 7
ankle 4
ankylosaurus 40
anorak 8
ant 31
antelope 37
apple 26
apricot 26
apron 20
arm 4
armchair 16
artichoke 24
asparagus 24
assembly toy 18
asteroid belt 44
astronaut 59
autumn 48
avocado 25

## B

baby food 28
back of the hand 4
backhoe loader 58
backpack 60
bacon 29
bactrian camel 36
badminton racket 68
bag 58
bag of cookies 28
bagel 28
baggage trailer 52
baguette 28
baking sheet 21
ball 11, 73
ballerina 75
balloon 72
ballpoint pen 61
banana 26
barley 33
barn 33
barrette 15
base 16
baseball 68
baseball glove 68
basket 53, 69
basketball 69
bathroom scale 14
bathtub 14
battery 71
beach 46
beach towel 38
beach umbrella 39
bean 25
bear 35
beaver 35

bedside table 13
beet 24
behind 7
bell 66
bell tower 56
belt 9
beside 7
bicycle 54
bicycle helmet 54
biplane 53
birch 34
bird feeder 43
birdhouse 43
birthday cake 72
black currants 27
blackberries 27
blackboard eraser 60
blender 20
blocks 18
blue 62
blue + red = purple 62
blueberries 26
blusher 15
boat 50
bobby pin 15
bone 5, 31
book 17
bookcase 17
boot 9
bow 50, 67
bowl 31
bowling ball 68
boxer shorts 9
brachiosaurus 40
brake 54
branch 30
branches 34
briefs 9
broccoli 24
brown sugar 23
brush 19
brussels sprouts 24
bubble bath 14
bucket 38
bucket swing 11
bud 43
budgie 30
bulletin board 60
bumblebee 31
bun 23
bus shelter 57
bush 42
business aircraft 53
butte 47
butter 28
butter dish 22
butterfly 31
butterfly fish 38
button 9

## C

cabbage 24
cabinet 20
cage 30
cake 23
calculator 60
calf 33
camp stove 70
campfire 70
can opener 21
canary 30
candies 29
candle 72
canoe 51
car 55
car wash 57
carambola 27

caravel 51
cardigan 8
cards 19
cargo aircraft 53
carnation 42
carrot 24
cash register 28
cassette 13
cassette player 17
castanets 67
cat 30
catamaran 50
cauliflower 24
cave 47
CD-radio-cassette player 13
CD/DVD drive 61
ceiling fixture 13
celery 24
cereal 23
chair 60
chalk 60
chalk board 60
chameleon 30
changing table 12
cheese 28
cherries 27
chick 32
chicken 29
chiffonier 13
chimney 11
chin 4
chipmunk 35
chives 25
chocolate bar 29
Christmas tree 73
chrysalis 31
church 56
cicada 31
circle 63
citrus juicer 21
city bus 55
clarinet 66
claw 36
cliff 46
clip 60
clock 60
cloud 49
cloud of volcanic ash 47
clown 75
clown fish 38
coat hooks 13
coconut 27
coffeemaker 20
colander 20
collar 9
colored pencils 19
comb 15
comet 45
comforter 12
compact disc 13, 61
compact disc player 17
compost bin 43
compressed-air cylinder 59
computer 61
condominiums 56
cone 63
confetti 72
container ship 51
control tower 52
controller 19
cooked ham 29
cookie cutters 21
cookies 23
cooler 71
corkscrew 21

corn 33
corncob 33
cotton applicators 14
counter 29
cow 32
cowboy 75
crab 39
crackers 72
cranberry 27
crater 47
crawl 6
crayons 19
creamer 22
crescent moon 44
crib 12
crocodile 37
crocus 42
croissant 28
cross-country skier 69
cry 7
cube 63
cucumber 25
cup 22, 70
curling iron 15
currant 27
curtain 12
cushion 16
cutlery set 70
cutting board 21
cylinder 63
cymbals 67

## D

daffodil 42
daisy 42
dandelion 42
darts 19
deer 35
deinonychus 40
dental floss 14
desert 47
dew 48
die 19
diplodocus 41
dishwasher 20
diskette 61
diskette drive 61
disposable razor 15
divided by 64
dog 31
doll 18
dolphin 39
dominoes 19
donkey 32
door 11, 13, 71
down 7
dragon 75
dragonfly 31
drawer 20
drawing board 18
dress 8
dresser 12
drive chain 54
driver 58
drizzle 49
dromedary camel 36
drum sticks 67
drums 67
dryer 15
duck 32
dune 47
duty belt 59
DVD 17
DVD player 17

## E

ear 4
Earth 44
easel 19, 63
Easter eggs 73

edger 10
egg 28
egg carton 28
eggplant 25
eight 64
elbow 4
electric guitar 67
electric range 21
electric razor 15
elephant 37
engine 52
equals 64
eraser 61
eraser holder 61
eye 4, 48
eyelash 4
eyelid 4
eyeshadow 15

## F

factory 57
fairy 74
falcon 35
fan 16
faucet 14
felt tip pen 19
fence 10
fennec 36
fennel 24
fern 34
field mouse 35
fig 27
figure skate 68
finger 4
fingernail 4
fins 38
fir 34
fire extinguisher 59
fire hose 59
fire hydrant 57
fire irons 17
fire station 56
fire truck 59
fire-fighting aircraft 53
firefighter 59
fireplace 16
fireworks 73
fish 23
five 64
flashlight 71
flat sheet 12
fleshy leaf 25
floor lamp 16
flour 23
flower 43
flower bud 43
flute 72
fly 8, 31
foam pad 70
fog 48
folding armchair 71
folding chairs 16
foliage 34
food can 28
foot 4
football 69
football player 69
footboard 12
fork 23, 33
fountain pen 61
four 64
freezer 20
freezer bag 28
freezing rain 49
frog 35
frost 49
fruit juice 28
frying pan 21, 70
full moon 44
funnel 21
funnel cloud 48
fuselage 52
futon 16

## G

galaxy 45
galley 51
Gallic warrior 75
game console 19
garage 11
garbage can 10
garden hose 10
gardening gloves 43
garland 73
garlic 25
gasoline pump 57
geographical map 60
gherkin 25
ghost 74
gift 73
gift bag 73
gift wrap 72
giraffe 37
glacier 46
glass 22
glider swing 11
globe 60
gloves 9
glue stick 19
gnome 74
goal 68
goat 32
goldfinch 35
goldfish 30
golf ball 69
golf club 69
goose 32
gorilla 37
grandfather clock 16
grapefruit 26
grapes 27
grasshopper 31
grater 21
gravy boat 22
green 62
green peas 25
greeting card 72
guinea pig 30
gull 39
gum 5

## H

hadrosaurus 40
hail 49
hair dryer 15
hairbrush 15
Halloween pumpkin 73
hammer 10
hamster 30
hand mixer 20
handlebars 54
hanger 12
hard hat 58
hare 35
harmonica 66
harp 66
hat 72
hatchet 59
head 4
headboard 12
headdress 73
headlight 55
headphones 17
heart 5
heavy rain 49
hedge 11
heel 8
helicopter 53
helmet 59, 69
hen 32
hen house 32
high-rise apartment building 56
highlighter pen 61

# Indice español